STYLE FOR STUDENTS:
Effective Writing in Science and Engineering

Joe Schall

College of Earth & Mineral Sciences
The Pennsylvania State University

 BURGESS INTERNATIONAL GROUP INC
Burgess Publishing

Address orders to:

BURGESS INTERNATIONAL GROUP, INC.
7110 Ohms Lane
Edina, Minnesota 55439-2143
Telephone 612/820-4561
Fax 612/831-3167

Burgess Publishing
A Division of BURGESS INTERNATIONAL GROUP, Inc.

*This book is for Bill,
my best teacher.*

Foreword

Most of us like to tell others about our really good ideas. We enjoy the excitement of talking about our thoughts, of seeing our listener reflect a new understanding. So we know that finding the right words to express ideas is rewarding, and we know that our vague thoughts or insights are not shaped into a final form until they are carefully sculpted into a compelling written or verbal presentation. Effective writing is particularly important in science and engineering where the need for clarity and precision is evident, and where the relationship between poor writing and muddled thought is hard to hide.

Believing that good communication skills can be learned and that they should be a vital part of the education of scientists and engineers, a few years ago we made a commitment to blend focused experiences in written and oral communication into our science and engineering courses. Penn State's College of Earth and Mineral Sciences is a particularly good setting for such an experiment, since our disciplines range from materials and mineral engineering, through earth and environmental sciences, to geography and economics—a spectrum that proved to be both an advantage and a challenge. We also enjoyed the enthusiastic support of our faculty and staff. Leaders of our professions endorsed our effort, stressing the importance they place on good communication skills when selecting people for positions of responsibility in their businesses and industries.

As part of our initiative, we engaged Joe Schall, a talented professional writer, to serve the college as full-time tutor and work closely with our students, helping them to write more effectively. Through personal interactions with our students, Joe discovered much about our students and their writing habits. He found that they respond favorably to certain approaches—they want examples of good and bad writing; they want to be shown alternative ways to express an idea; they appreciate lists of acceptable words that emphasize the options available to them; they want models they can study; and above all they respond to teaching designed for their own discipline. Time and again they came back to learn more and try again. Joe's teaching had its effect.

Seeing his success, we asked Joe to put his ideas into words, to create a manual that would help students learn to write more effectively. Here is the result—*Style for Students*.

John A. Dutton, Dean
College of Earth and Mineral Sciences

ABOUT THE AUTHOR

Joe Schall is the writing tutor for the College of Earth and Mineral Sciences at Penn State University. He specializes in working one-on-one with undergraduate scientists and engineers. He received an M.A. in English from Penn State in 1988 and a B.S. in English Education from Juniata College in 1981. He also writes fiction, and his first collection of short stories, *Indentation and Other Stories,* won the 1990 Bobst Award for Emerging Writers from the New York University Library. He resides in State College, Pennsylvania, with his wife Elisabeth Rose and their daughter Delaney.

AUTHOR'S ACKNOWLEDGMENTS

My abundant thanks to all those who helped me to complete this manual, either by offering formal critique, providing me with models, or lending moral support. I owe particular thanks to Dean John Dutton, who supported this project from the beginning and read every word I supplied, and Dr. Craig Bohren, who gave me a generous amount of spirited advice. Dean John Cahir, Dr. Peter Thrower, Mrs. Judy Kiusalaas, Dr. Earle Ryba, Mrs. Sandi Grenci, and Dr. Joan Parrett also gave plenty of meaningful counsel. Much of the material in Chapter 7 was adapted from resources generously provided by the Penn State University Libraries. Finally, I warmly acknowledge all those students whose writing I chose to showcase as positive models in this book, in particular Thomas Davinroy, Peter Beckage, Charles Long, Julie Gulick, Jill Coakley, Christopher Marino, Katharine Butler, Shana Gordon, Andrew Hoover, Andrew Campbell, Shepard Winckler, Thomas Gebbie, Kirsten Laarkamp, Kim Kelly, and Stephen Shierloh.

COMMENTS ON THIS MANUAL

Any comments on or questions about this manual can be directed to the author:

Joe Schall
College of Earth and Mineral Sciences
116 Deike Building
University Park, PA 16802

Office phone: 814-863-6077
FAX: 814-863-7708
e-mail: u3w@psuvm.psu.edu

Contents

Foreword   *V*
Preface   *XIV*
Introduction   *1*

Chapter 1: *Writing-Intensive Courses*   **5**

OUTLINES   **5**
The Value of Outlining   6
Mechanics of Outlining   6
Sample Outline   7

ANNOTATED BIBLIOGRAPHIES   **8**
Style for Annotated Bibliographies   8
Sample Annotated Bibliography   9

DESCRIPTIVE ABSTRACTS   **10**
Style for Descriptive Abstracts   10
Sample Descriptive Abstract   11

PROPOSALS   **12**
Pitfalls of Proposals   13
Style for Proposals   13
Sample Proposal   14

PROGRESS REPORTS   **15**
Style for Progress Reports   16
Sample Progress Report   17

MEMOS   **18**
A Memo About Memo Writing   18

ESSAYS AND TERM PAPERS   **20**
Mechanics   20
Title   20
Introduction   20
Thesis Statement / Objective   21
Body Paragraphs / Section Headings   22
Conclusion   22
References   23

TECHNICAL REPORTS   **23**
Mechanics   24
Title   24
Abstract   24
Introduction   25

Literature Review   25
Experimental / Methods / Procedures   26
Results   27
Discussion   27
Conclusions   27
Acknowledgments   28
References   28
Appendices   28

ORAL REPORTS   **28**
Preparation and General Presentation   29
Visual Aids   30
Your Manner As You Speak   31

Chapter 2: *Improving Your Style* 33

CONCISION, PRECISION, REVISION   **33**

SUBJECT/VERB AGREEMENT   **35**

TRICKY SINGULAR/PLURAL PAIRS   **36**

VERB TENSE   **37**

WHAT MAKES A PARAGRAPH TICK?   **38**
Four Methods For Writing Good Paragraphs   38

TOPIC SENTENCES   **39**

TRANSITION WORDS   **40**

USING ACTIVE VERBS   **41**
Active Verbs That Describe Work   41
Using Verbs To Describe Phenomena   42
Active Verbs That Describe Phenomena   43

THE PASSIVE/ACTIVE VOICE DILEMMA   **43**

WHEN TO USE THE ACTIVE VOICE   **45**

WHEN TO USE THE PASSIVE VOICE   **46**

COMMONLY OVERUSED WORDS   **47**
Will, Would, Can, Could   47
Aspects   48
"This" And "It"   49
Feelings   50

SPECIAL STYLISTIC CONVENTIONS OF SCIENCE AND ENGINEERING **50**
Avoiding Sexist Language   50
Beware of Dangling Modifiers   51
Unsplitting Infinitives   52

Contractions Not Welcome   52
Textual References To Temperature Measurements   53
Textual References To Numbers   53

Chapter 3: *Punctuation, Capitalization, and Spelling*   55

QUOTATION MARKS   56

HYPHENS   56

SEMICOLONS, COLONS, AND DASHES   57
The Semicolon   57
The Colon   58
The Dash   58

COMMAS   58
Comma Rules   59
The Comma Before an "And" Dilemma   60
Killing the Comma   60

CAPITALIZATION   61

COMMON CAPITALIZATION ERRORS   63

SPELL CHECKING   63

SPELLING RULES   64

COMMONLY MISSPELLED WORDS   66

COMMONLY MISSPELLED TERMINOLOGY   69

Chapter 4: *Commonly Misused Terms*   71

Accept/Except   71
Affect/Effect   71
Alot   72
Alright   72
Alternate/Alternative   72
Among/Between   72
Amount of/Number of   73
Area/Region/Section   73
As/Like   73
Assure/Ensure/Insure   73
Between . . . and/From . . . to/—   74
Cite/Site/Sight   74
Compare to/Compare with   74
Compose/Constitute/Include   74
Comprise   75
Continual/Continuous   75

Different than/Different from 75
e.g./et al./i.e. 75
etc. 76
Fact/Factor 76
Farther/Further 76
Fewer/Less 76
Imply/Infer 77
In terms of 77
Irregardless 77
It's/Its 77
Lay/Lie 78
Lead/Led 78
May/Might 78
One/You 78
Per 79
Percent/Percentage 79
Pretty/Quite/Rather/Very 79
Principal/Principle 79
Respective/Respectively 79
s / 's 80
That/Which 80
Try and 80

Chapter 5: *Equations, Figures, and Tables* 81

EQUATIONS 81
Style for Equations 82
Sample Equation 83

FIGURES AND TABLES 83
Textual References to Figures and Tables 84
Aesthetics for Figures and Tables 85
Captions for Figures and Tables 85
Fundamentals for Figures 86
Fundamentals for Tables 86
Sample Figure 87
Sample Table 88

Chapter 6: *Using Sources* 91

FUNDAMENTALS OF USING SOURCES 92

WHEN SOURCES *MUST* BE CITED 93

INTEGRATING YOUR SOURCES 94

ANATOMY OF A WELL-DOCUMENTED PARAGRAPH 95

THE AUTHOR-YEAR SYSTEM OF DOCUMENTATION 97
   Sample Author-Year Citations 97
   Style For The References Page—Author-Year System 97
   Special References Page Dilemmas 98
   Sample References Page—Author-Year System 98

THE NUMBER SYSTEM OF DOCUMENTATION 99
   Sample Number System Citations 99
   Style For The References Page—Number System 99
   Special References Page Dilemmas 100
   Sample References Page—Number System 100

AN IMPORTANT WORD ABOUT REFERENCES PAGES 101

Chapter 7: *Library Resources*   *103*

STYLE MANUALS 104

GENERAL RESOURCES FOR SCIENCE AND ENGINEERING 106

EARTH SCIENCE RESOURCES 107

MATERIALS SCIENCE RESOURCES 108

MINERAL ECONOMICS AND MINERAL ENGINEERING RESOURCES 109

LIFE SCIENCE RESOURCES 110

CHEMISTRY AND CHEMICAL ENGINEERING RESOURCES 111

MATHEMATICAL SCIENCE RESOURCES 112

PHYSICS AND ASTRONOMY RESOURCES 113

AEROSPACE, MECHANICAL, ELECTRICAL, AND NUCLEAR ENGINEERING
   RESOURCES 114

ENVIRONMENTAL, ARCHITECTURAL, AGRICULTURAL, INDUSTRIAL,
   AND CIVIL ENGINEERING RESOURCES 115

Chapter 8: *Resumes, Letters, and Graduate School Application Essays*   *117*

WRITING RESUMES 118
   Overall Mechanical Guidelines 118
   Name and Addresses 119
   Objective 119
   Education 120
   Experience / Work Experience / Employment 120
   Activities / Honors / Professional Activities 121
   References 121
   Creating Your Own Category 122
   The Graduate Student Resume 122

LIST OF COMMON ACTION WORDS   **123**

SAMPLE RESUME FOR AN INTERNSHIP   **125**

SAMPLE RESUME   **126**

SAMPLE RESUME   **127**

SAMPLE RESUME   **128**

SAMPLE GRADUATE STUDENT RESUME   **129**

PROFESSIONAL LETTERS   **131**
Overall Mechanical Guidelines   131
The Heading and Greeting   132
The Opening Paragraph   132
The Middle Paragraph(s)   132
The Closing Paragraph and Graceful Exit   133

STATE TWO-LETTER ABBREVIATIONS   **133**

SAMPLE "TAILORED" COVER LETTER   **134**

SAMPLE "BLIND" COVER LETTER   **135**

SAMPLE "BLIND" COVER LETTER FOR AN INTERNSHIP   **136**

SAMPLE "SKILLS" COVER LETTER   **137**

SAMPLE THANK YOU LETTER   **138**

SAMPLE LETTER ACKNOWLEDGING A JOB OFFER   **139**

SAMPLE LETTER ACCEPTING A JOB OFFER   **140**

GRADUATE SCHOOL APPLICATION ESSAYS   **141**
Answer Each Part Of The Essay Question Explicitly   141
Choose A Narrative, Research, Or A Teaching Approach   141
Discuss Your Background Concretely And Professionally   141
Learn All You Can About The Program You Are Applying To   141

SAMPLE GRADUATE SCHOOL APPLICATION ESSAY — RESEARCH APPROACH   **143**

SAMPLE GRADUATE SCHOOL APPLICATION ESSAY — NARRATIVE APPROACH   **144**

REQUESTING RECOMMENDATION LETTERS   **145**
Think Through the Application Process First   145
Use Application Materials to Help You Choose
    Recommenders   145
Seek a Mix of Recommenders, and Identify Their Roles
    for Them   145
Choose Recommenders Who Know You Well and Help
    Them to Know You Better   145
Respect a "No"   145

Allow the Letter to be Confidential and Let the
  Recommender Discuss Your Grades   145
Provide the Recommender with a Firm Deadline
  and a Stamped Addressed Envelope   146
Begin to Recognize Yourself as a Professional   146

TIPS FOR INTERVIEWS   **147**
What To Do   147
What Not To Do   147
Qualities That You Should Enhance in an Interview   147
The Top Reasons Why Job Seekers Are Rejected   147

Chapter 9: *Journal Articles About Writing*   **149**

COMMENTS FROM SOME MIFFED EDITORS   **150**

EVEN MORE COMMENTS FROM THE SAME MIFFED EDITORS   **153**

THE SCIENCE OF SCIENTIFIC WRITING   **156**

ADVICE TO SCIENTIST-WRITERS: BEWARE OLD 'FALLACIES'   **157**

THE UNIVERSAL RECIPE FOR SCIENTIFIC REPORTS   **160**
Overview   160
Title   161
Authorship   162
Abstract   162
Introduction   163
Experimental section   165
Results section   165
Discussion section   166
Conclusions (or Summary and Conclusions) section   167
Acknowledgments section   167
References Cited section   168

A BIBLIOGRAPHY OF ADDITIONAL JOURNAL ARTICLES ABOUT WRITING   **169**
Anatomy and Physiology   170
Biology   170
Business   170
Chemistry   170
Engineering   171
Mathematics   171
Music   172
Nursing/Medicine   172
Physics   172
Sociology   172
Writing in the Sciences and Engineering in General   173

REFERENCES CITED   **175**
INDEX   **177**

Preface

This is a work of serendipity. An unexpected gift to me from my students. After years of sharing advice about writing I was compelled to write some of it down. What is especially gratifying me for is witnessing those in technical fields as they grow excited about writing. A student and I sit together at a table, we look down at a piece of paper, we look up at each other and discuss the writing before us, the computer hums nearby, and suddenly something lights up for both of us. That is what I hope this manual will do for students—illuminate the waiting overhead bulb.

And to those who responded so favorably and helpfully to earlier versions of this manual, I hope these pages further kindle your already heightened appreciation for writing. Thanks to word-of-mouth and a small innocent-looking note in Penn State's College of Earth and Mineral Sciences bulletin, Earth & Mineral Sciences, we received requests for a copy of earlier versions of this manual from dozens of people, ranging from professors at the University of Calabar, Nigeria, and the University of Auckland, New Zealand, to a journal editor in Canada, a Chief Engineer for the United States Army, and a Chief Meteorologist at NASA.

All of this interest in the manual has made me appreciate just how much scientists and engineers care about exactitude, especially in writing. Perhaps the most delightful and indicative response to an earlier version of this manual came from the Permanent Secretary of the Ministry of Energy and Energy Industries in Trinidad. My surprise at his long-distance lunch-time phone call was equaled only by my appreciation as he kindly and quietly told me that he thought I should know I had misspelled a particular author's name. And he was, of course, correct.

Joe Schall
May, 1995

Introduction

*I always find that statistics are hard to swallow
and impossible to digest. The only one I can ever
remember is that if all the people who go to sleep in
church were laid end to end they would all be a lot
more comfortable.*

　　　　　　　　　　　　　　　　—Mrs. Robert A Taft

At some point, each of us has probably had the unhappy surprise
of receiving a graded paper decorated with an army of what
look to be squiggly red ants swarming over the pages, probably
prompting us to say, usually to a roommate, friend, or a parent, "My
teacher just doesn't like my style." When our writing is criticized and
graded, it is tempting to think that the grader simply does not like our
way of writing (especially if we went to the trouble of using a spell-
checker and consulting a thesaurus a few times). In hard terms,
though, style has to do with everything from the denotations and connotations of the words we choose to the flow of our paragraphs to the
quality of our proofreading. If we write with grace, clarity, and grammatical correctness we are rewarded, while if we write with sloppi-
ness, obscurity, and improper grammar we are criticized. This manual
is about helping you to be rewarded for your style.

Now allow me to be pithy and preachy for a moment. The
American Industrial Writing Institute tells us that the technically
trained person is too often a poor writer. In fact, studies confirm what
executives and writing teachers have been saying for a long time: out
of every 100 engineers, about 5 can write well (1). What surprises
many students after graduation is that they end up doing quite a bit of
writing on the job—in fact, those in managerial positions do the most
writing of all, and they are expected to have superior communication
skills. Memos, letters of transmittal, grant proposals, journal articles,
feasibility studies, speeches, progress reports, public relations pieces:
all of these can be as much a part of the scientist's or engineer's routine as the reading of logs or the analysis of data. Case in point: 245
people listed in Engineers of Distinction said that they devote one-
fourth of their time on the job to writing (2). A 1983 M.I.T. study of
engineers and scientists at Exxon Chemical Company showed that
technical professionals typically spend over a third of their work week
preparing oral reports, writing, or editing (3). In 1980, Nicholas D.
Sylvester, the Dean of Engineering and Physical Sciences and Director
of the Petroleum and Energy Research Institute at the University of

Tulsa, estimated that as engineers move up the managerial ladder, as much as 80 percent of their time can be spent in the writing/reporting process (4). Writers of technical information are also in the position of having either a highly specific or a surprisingly varied audience for their work, and thus they must consciously attend to the needs of such an audience.

So what does your audience want? In scientific writing, the answer is simple: speedy comprehension and precise information, and the two go hand in hand. Our sentences must be understood rapidly and easily so that our audience can use the information that our words convey, and we need to remember as we write that our audience wants us to write well. There is a growing amount of evidence that professional organizations care greatly about good writing. Both Mobil and the Mining and Metallurgical Society of America, just to name two, sponsor student writing contests with first-prize cash awards of $1,000. Medical organizations are now sponsoring week-long mountain-lodge retreats packed with writing seminars designed for doctors who want to become better writers. Recently, a student applying for an entry-level position with the Department of Energy told me that, as part of her on-site interview, she was given 20 minutes to write a short essay describing her background for a managerial position. I know of at least one meteorology service and one environmental engineering firm that require a ten-page writing sample when you apply for a job.

Good writing also matters because it gives you credibility; it tells your readers to take you seriously, to trust you. The chemist who fails to describe the apparatus clearly in the "Experimental" section of a scientific report has let the reader down; the hydrologist who writes "Some land surface was effected in a cylindrical-like container of H_2O" instead of "We dropped some mud in a glass of water" is being needlessly verbose and complex. The sentence—"As a cashier, my supervisor was satisfied with me"—which recently appeared on a resume, literally means that the supervisor was the cashier. And the following sentence from a composition paper on voluntary euthanasia was downright embarrassing for the writer: "If a person is a vegetable, it is fruitless to try to keep him alive on a machine." Here is another genuine gem that I once encountered in a student's paper: "One who is the victim of a motorcycle accident would have a lot less trouble in terms of not wearing his helmet if he would only use his head while driving." (My translation: "Wear your cycle helmet.")

Now I will get more picky, as your teachers are bound to do. Suppose you are a student in meteorology. Referring to temperatures as "high" and "low" is much more acceptable than calling them "warm" and "cool" or "hot" and "cold." Dr. Craig Bohren, Distinguished Professor of Meteorology at Penn State, sums up the reasoning for this rule in an amusing fashion: "Let us have warm hearts, give warm regards, and form warm friendships. Let us experience warm fronts and, as winter approaches, even warm behinds. But please, no more warm temperatures . . . To say that a temperature rather than an object is warm or cold is to blur the distinction between an attribute and its measure. It is like saying that an IQ score is stupid or smart" (5). This is just one example of how one or two key words misused can matter dramatically to a reader in your discipline. No doubt most teachers of meteorology would cringe to hear a meteorologist on the Weather Channel merrily announce, "For the weekend, we're talkin' warm temperatures."

Further, suppose a biologist writes "absorb" when "adsorb" is correct, or a petroleum engineer continually misspells "reservoir," or a mining student's spell-checker does not realize that "too cool seems" is really supposed to be "two coal seams." Does it matter to your readers? You bet it does. Such stylistic flaws not only drop you down a peg in your graded writing, they irritate your educated readers and breed disrespect. The bottom line is always the same: write well and you prosper; write poorly and you flounder, or you do not even get read.

This manual is here to help you. It is a practical writing toolkit that you can carry with you through your academic studies and beyond. As positive models for your own writing, I give you sentences and paragraphs written by your peers. About 95 percent of the positive example sentences, paragraphs, and longer documents in this manual are taken directly from papers written by students in the College of Earth and Mineral Sciences at Penn State—evidence of how much student writers can learn from each other. You are bound to have English textbooks on your shelves that will prove to be handy references as well—that is why they have indexes.

Stylish writing takes time and careful work; for most people it requires a lot of revision. I gave what I hoped was a final draft of this manual to some professors at Penn State and some other friends for their critique, and one of my colleagues typed me a fourteen-page reply. I recall one of my original phrases that I was particularly in love with, about sentences "inhabiting airspace," and two meteorologists, one metallurgist, and my teenage neighbor were quick to inform me that sentences did not and never would "inhabit airspace." I was revising for a long time. This Introduction took me over 20 hours to complete and it was almost the last part of the manual that I wrote. The first sentence alone gobbled up 40 minutes. As I analyze the style of the Introduction I find that I took aim at my audience by choosing words that would foster both a chatty and a serious tone, by drawing concrete examples from both the general scientific community and my tutoring experiences at Penn State, by exploiting all sorts of punctuation marks and sentence options, and by sticking to one simple topic per paragraph. For me, these tactics illustrate just how many options our language offers us. I also took notes for the final few paragraphs as I composed the first few paragraphs, realizing as I wrote what ideas I wanted to save for my closing. Lastly, I had the luxury of setting this manual aside for a few years and then revising it completely, and I ended up changing about 40 percent of the text overall and about 30 percent of the text in the Introduction alone. I went to all this trouble to try to convince you that using this manual will be immediately fruitful. So read on. Good things await you.

Chapter 1

Writing-Intensive Courses

If you have a job without aggravations, you don't have a job.
—Malcolm Forbes

As a user of this manual, you are probably enrolled in a writing-intensive course (also called w-courses or writing-across-the-curriculum courses). In a nutshell, the aim of these courses is to help you learn about a subject by researching and writing about it, and in some courses you actually produce the kinds of documents that are common to your discipline beyond graduation. Some writing-intensive courses require a series of short assignments culminating in a longer report, while others require both oral and written presentation and are akin to a senior thesis. In any case, all writing-intensive courses provide you with ample opportunity to receive concrete feedback on your writing from your professor.

All that said, it must be noted that, from both the professor's and student's point of view, writing-intensive courses often mean extra work and higher standards. Yet many professors are happy to teach them, because it becomes clear from the course's very definition that good communication skills are key to good science, or good engineering, or good business. While you may groan at the prospect of both the workload and standards of a writing-intensive course, they do serve to underscore the fact that writing will matter greatly in any profession you choose.

Simply put, this chapter is designed to help you survive writing-intensive courses. Individual sections in this chapter are devoted to the types of forms you will probably be using in any course in science and engineering, whether it is designated as writing-intensive or not. By reviewing the stylistic tips and the models herein, and following any advice your professor gives to the letter, you should be able not just to breathe a little easier in any writing-intensive course that you take, but to thrive.

Outlines

Most students see outlines as a royal pain. But not only are they often central to writing-intensive courses, they are frequently required on the job; for example, a project manager may require each individual team member to outline and compose different portions of a joint report. Do not be seduced by the belief that an outline is totally useless or simply mechanical; this will only be true if you make it so.

The Value of Outlining

Let us begin by understanding the utility of outlines. They foster coherence by helping the writer to:

- plan both the sequence and hierarchy of information.

- make decisions about organization and content without the distraction of all the details of composition.

- avoid repetition, digression, poor emphasis, and poor flow.

- improve general organizational skills.

Considered in the light of the above ideal, outlines can be as fundamental to the writer as a flowchart is to the computer programmer. Also, keep in mind that outlines can be, by definition, somewhat rough and speculative. They must still be concrete and reader-centered, of course, but good writers use outlines to flesh out their ideas, organize their thoughts, and discover their gaps. As long as the mechanics of the outline are correct and the details concrete, most professors will not be too finicky about the quality of your outlining skills, and will simply take the opportunity to give you quick feedback on your ideas and organization.

Mechanics of Outlining

The mechanics of outlining are simple. The two most common forms used are the Arabic System and the Decimal System. Indentations of a tab (1/2-inch or five spaces) are used to designate hierarchy of material, and order is indicated by sequential numbers, letters, or Roman numerals. What follows is a simple depiction of the two systems:

DECIMAL SYSTEM

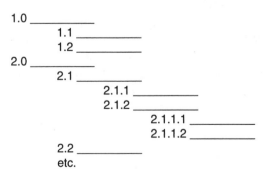

```
1.0 _____
          1.1 _____
          1.2 _____
2.0 _____
          2.1 _____
                    2.1.1 _____
                    2.1.2 _____
                              2.1.1.1 _____
                              2.1.1.2 _____
          2.2 _____
          etc.
```

ARABIC SYSTEM

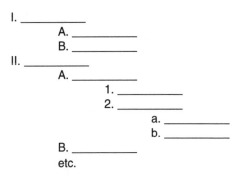

I. _____
     A. _____
     B. _____
II. _____
     A. _____
         1. _____
         2. _____
             a. _____
             b. _____
     B. _____
     etc.

Note how the Decimal System requires a period between numbers, and note that, for both systems, the rising sequence of the numbers, letters, or Roman numerals is determined by the level of the heading under which a character falls.

Sample Outline

The sample outline that follows is a perfect example of how a writer can use an outline as an effective organizational tool. This outline was prepared by a student writing his senior thesis. Note how the outline is both highly focused yet openly speculative; the writer even goes so far as to make comments to himself, and even though he does not fine-tune each thought nor know the exact results of his study at the time of writing, he is organized, thoughtful, and specific.

Working Title: "The Search for Folding in the GISP Ice Core"
by Shepard Winckler

Abstract
I. Introduction
   A. Background
      1. Interest in global climate records for future predictions.
      2. Description of the GISP project.
         a. Location, depth, time covered, etc.
         b. Possibly some historical info. on other cores.
   B. Discussion of recently published articles by European paleoclimatologists.
      1. Their interpretation of the Eemain interglacial stage.
      2. My argument about their theories, which warrants my study.
         a. Recent interest in folding and its effects on the ice record.
         b. Fluctuations in temperature for this stage found deep in the core.
         c. At this depth ice has the potential to fold, thus distorting the record.
   C. Information on up-indicators.
      1. Other uses of up-indicators in geology and their dependability.
      2. Possible indicators in the ice record.
         a. Dust in core (laser scattering).
         b. Acids in core (ecm data).

II. Detailed Objective of Study
  A. Search for up-indicators in the ice record.
    1. Search for consistent asymmetry of peaks in the graphical record.
  B. If peaks are consistently asymmetric, then look for a reverse of symmetry at depth.
    1. If symmetry is reversed, then the ice has been overturned.
    2. If no reversal of symmetry, this method is unusable.
  C. Possible objective of interpreting the record of the Eemain interglacial.
III. Methods of the Study
  A. Measurement of the dust and ecm data graphical peaks.
  B. Calculation of the symmetry (or asymmetry) of the peaks.
  C. Test for statistical dependability.
IV. Results
  A. Was there a statistically consistent asymmetry?
  B. Was folding discovered using the dust and ecm data as an up-indicator?
V. Conclusion
  A. Response to European theories.
  B. Dependability of this study method.
  C. Some interpretation of my own.
VI. References.

Annotated Bibliographies

Many professors ask you to write annotated bibliographies—bibliographic information about your primary sources and a short description of each—as preparation for writing a paper. Often, these bibliographies are no more than a page or two in length, but they are important because they force you to get your teeth into the source material and they give your professor the opportunity to comment on your use of sources and suggest sources that you may have overlooked.

Style for Annotated Bibliographies

- Begin by listing complete bibliographic information (author, year, source name, publisher, etc.) just as you would on the References page at the end of a paper.

- Provide a sentence or two describing the contents of the source.

- Summarize the various relevant topic areas that the source discusses.

- Avoid vague phrasing and empty sentences. Weed out any generic sentences such as "This source is very useful because it has tons of really good information."

- Use present tense and future tense verbs to facilitate the immediacy of the information and the actual future use of sources.

- Discuss the exact way that you will use the source (e.g., for background information, data, graphics, as a bibliographic tool).

- Carefully judge the value of the source, considering, for example, its level of detail, bias, or the timeliness of its data.

- Note if the source's text or bibliography will lead you to other sources.

- Comment on anything that you find especially unique about a source—is it controversial? definitive? new? political?

- Format the annotated bibliography so that each description is clearly associated with the proper source.

Sample Annotated Bibliography

An excellent annotated bibliography by a geography student follows. Note how he takes advantage of all of the stylistic advice above, and how the paper's sections are beginning to take shape even in the source descriptions.

ANNOTATED BIBLIOGRAPHY
"The Geography of American Graveyards"

by Andrew Campbell

Jordan, Terry G. (1982). *Texas Graveyards, A Cultural Legacy.* Austin: University of Texas Press.

Jordan offers an in-depth look at the hows and whys of Texas graveyards. He divides vernacular burial sites into three categories: Mexican, German, and "Southern folk cemeteries." His physical descriptions of cemetery layout, inscriptions, grave markers, and the like are very detailed.

Meyer, Richard E., ed. (1989). *Cemeteries and Gravemarkers, Voices of American Culture.* Ann Arbor: UMI Research Press.

Meyer's book is a compilation of works concerning such topics as regional epitaphs, origins of Southern cemeteries, the Afro-American section of a Rhode Island burial ground, and the use of bronze in memorials.

Sloane, David Charles (1991). *The Last Great Necessity, Cemeteries in American History.* Baltimore: the Johns Hopkins University Press.

Sloane's work will serve as my primary source of information. He has written a history of American cemeteries in a cultural context, concentrating on significant trends in their development. Sloane's "Notes" section will allow for easy access to other sources.

Weed, Howard Evarts (1912). *Modern Park Cemeteries.* Chicago: R.J. Haight.

Weed was a landscape architect and his work concentrates on how a cemetery should look. Weed offers detailed descriptions of the physical layout of pre-20th century cemeteries.

Zelinsky, Wilbur (1994). "Gathering Places for America's Dead," *The Professional Geographer.* 46:1, 29-38.

Zelinsky's article is an intriguing analysis of the spatial patterns of American cemeteries. He calculates and maps the number of cemeteries by county across the country. He then seeks answers as to why there is such a fluctuation in the number per square mile from one place to the next. Zelinsky's bibliography led me to Sloane's work.

Descriptive Abstracts

A Descriptive Abstract—a summary of someone else's paper or book—is often required by professors to give you practice in summarizing and responding to sources. Writing an abstract can be especially trying if you feel as though you are reading something over your head; however, if you understand the goals of a descriptive abstract precisely you can read and write in such a way that the author's ideas are simplified yet represented fairly.

Style for Descriptive Abstracts

- Include a title and the word "Abstract" as a heading. Include basic bibliographic information after the title (author's name, title of work, etc.).

- Frequently, a list of key words that will be used appears just underneath the title of the abstract. Consider listing your key words in this way.

- Many professors will expect you to limit a descriptive abstract to a single page, so be certain to write with efficiency in mind—no filler.

- Begin the abstract by providing some condensed background information and a statement of overview or purpose, much like the kind of material an author provides in an introduction and a thesis statement.

- Decide on topics by selecting key information from your source. Use the chapter headings, section headings, conclusions, topic sentences, and key terms from your source to determine the topics.

- Point out relationships among topics, especially via transition words.

- Consider working from an outline to organize and write the abstract.

- Use paragraphing generously to discuss different facets of the topic; do not fear short paragraphs.

- Consider techniques such as enumeration or bulleting of key points for emphasis. However, do not use section headings in an abstract.

- Use present tense verbs generously, both to describe ideas or events and to present the author's goals.

- Use the author's name or the names of other key authors, especially those who represent particular theories, directly in the text. However, do not cite sources in the abstract itself; the reader understands that all of the ideas in a descriptive abstract come from a particular source unless you note otherwise.

- Do not skimp on the conclusion; assert what the bottom line of the source is.

- Some professors will expect you or allow you to close the descriptive abstract with your own views on the subject or on the author's treatment of the subject. Explore this option as concretely you can.

- Do not use the abstract as a vehicle of apology for ideas you do not understand; stick to those key ideas that you can represent with precision.

Sample Descriptive Abstract

The sample abstract that follows is a solid model written for a class in mineral policy analysis. Note that, in accordance with her professor's guidelines, the writer gives her particular views on the author's treatment of the subject at the end of her descriptive abstract.

ABSTRACT
"Oil and National Security," by Darwin C. Hall, in
Energy Policy (1992) v. 20, no. 11

submitted by Karen Ziegenfus

Keywords: National Energy Security (NES), Strategic Petroleum Reserve (SPR), energy security, oil.

In February 1992, President Bush presented the National Energy Strategy (NES), which is based upon the ideals of a free market. Included in the NES are policies that remove restrictions on oil production and restrictions on the construction of nuclear power. This paper attempts to quantify the costs associated with spending on oil imports as related to national security and the Strategic Petroleum Reserve (SPR).

Energy security is measured by the size of U.S. imports because the Middle East holds the majority of reserves and oil reserves are being depleted. The consequence of this is that oil prices can be manipulated to harm the U.S. and its allies. Oil price shocks or supply disruptions instigated by OPEC cause recessions by lowering output, raising prices, and lowering real wages. These effects are determined by applying the Granger causality tests.

A benefit of a market-driven price determination system is that prices rise as depletable resources fall, implying increased scarcity. This rise in price gives an incentive to produce substitutes as well as reduce consumption of oil.

There is a large divergence between the social cost of energy and the price because of environmental externalities associated with conventional energy sources. The philosophy of the administration is to rely on market prices to determine 20 % of the economy's investment. However, misplaced investments based on such a policy have implications for many years. Hall concludes that the policies reflected in the NES will result in gross economic inefficiency.

I agree with Hall's conclusion that misplaced investment in such a large part of our economy is dangerous. I believe that there should be more of an analysis concerning how varying oil prices can affect the costs associated with oil import spending. This would show how vulnerable oil import spending is relative to price changes. Although Hall mentions the opportunity cost of interest that could have been earned had the amount spent been invested, he does not attempt to quantify what that amount is. I would attempt to calculate these costs using various interest rates. I also feel that he should calculate the inventory holding cost, and I am also curious to know what the cost of oil deterioration is and if there are transportation costs involved. These additional costs could be very significant in adding to the costs that Hall has already predicted.

Proposals

In the working world, you will often be in the position of writing a proposal, usually to try to solve a problem or receive approval or funding for a project. Such proposals must be prepared to exact specifications and must strike an artful balance between your own needs and those of your audience. Recently I worked closely with a professor as she prepared a proposal for some vital funding for her research, and her revisions during our discussion were effective because they were completely audience-centered and goal-oriented, even to the point that she revised tentative-sounding phrases into positive affirmations, shortened paragraphs and provided more transitions so that her sentences were easier to read and rescan, and changed certain past-tense verbs to present tense to establish more of a sense of exigence, or immediate relevance.

In writing-intensive courses, your professor may simply ask you to write a short topic proposal for his or her approval, or you may be asked to write an extensive proposal as a complete warm-up for a term paper. The advice that follows will help you prepare an extensive proposal.

Pitfalls of Proposals

When you are faced with the task of preparing a proposal for a paper, consider your audience's position first. Believe me, when a professor asks you to write a proposal, what he or she wants to do is read and understand it rapidly, perhaps give some feedback, and then grant speedy approval to someone who is clearly prepared to begin writing a paper. Empty phrases, vague detail, apparent self-absorption, cockiness, or a lack of confidence on your part just get in the way of all that. I once reviewed a batch of paper proposals in which the following sentences appeared verbatim:

> Another aspect in which I will ultimately show there is some importance here is...

> Currently I am working hard at gathering more information and also reviewing all of the present information, maps, and resources that I have etc., etc.

> At this point in time my proposed topic that I have given careful thought to and chosen for this paper is...

> By the deadline of this paper I will have expected myself to have gone far more into depth about this interesting topic and would have all of the required information.

Guess what? These writers do not exactly look prepared, do they? In the nearly 90 words above, there is absolutely nothing of use to the reader of the proposal, who wants specifics, not fluff. Windy phrases merely waste the reader's time and even breed suspicion that the writer has no real specifics to report. If you complicate what should be simple with such bloated, undigestible, and unswallowable phrases, your poor professor only winds up with a headache and heartburn.

Style for Proposals

- Try out a title.

- Include an immediately relevant introduction that briefly sets the context. Do not bother with such things as "Hi!!! Happy to be in your class. My name is Joseph. My social security number is . . . ."

- Have a premise, objective, or rationale clearly stated. Label it as such.

- Use brief, logical, concrete section headings to orient yourself and your reader.

- Take advantage of enumeration or formatting so that your important points stand out. Consider some sort of outline form where appropriate, even if only for one section of the proposal. Make it easy to scan.

- Do not waste any time at all. No verbal drumrolls.

- In general, do not hesitate to use "I," but do not overuse it. Sound like a person, even if it means taking a tiny stab at something that feels creative or bold. You may strike just the right human chord and be invited to do so in your paper as well.

- Pose questions. Actively speculate. Be thinking on the page.

- Remember that a proposal is not an absolute contract, but a thoughtful plan. Be specific about the work that you have not yet done as well as the work that you have. For example: "I am still speculating about how best to define the general characteristics of particle systems, and I know that I need to find more information on particle interactions, mechanics, and processing." Such a comment might inspire a helpful professor to jot a concrete note about where to find the needed information.

- Cite sources in your proposal, using the same citation style that you will use in the paper. You may be expected to give an annotated bibliography, but even if not, consider giving a sentence or so of description about your sources to establish your credibility, show the relevance of your initial research, and begin to spark the thoughts that the sources will help you to generate.

- Proofread the proposal with care, just as you should the final product.

Sample Proposal

What follows are excerpts from a proposal for a paper on the rapid growth of convenience store chains in America. Note how admirably the proposal takes advantage of all of the tips noted above. Also note that because the proposal author took the initiative to go to a convenience store chain's business office she found out that the chain had an historian, who provided her with abundant and excellent data, such as exit polls, to supplement her library research. This proposal was submitted by an earth science student and received enthusiastic approval and concrete feedback from the professor.

PROPOSAL for
"The Burgeoning of Convenience Stores Across the American Landscape"
by Katharine Butler

EXCERPT FROM THE "INTRODUCTION"

In a little over two decades we have witnessed the emergence of a new concept in retail buying for the American consumer—the convenience store. The United States government defines convenience stores as "food retailer(s) of limited lines in a freestanding sales area of 3,000 square feet, concentrating on selected fast-moving products" *(Directory of Supermarkets, Grocery, and Convenience Store Chains, 1990)*. To this definition I would add that typically the products on the shelves of convenience stores are priced higher than those carried by their competitors.

EXCERPT FROM THE "RATIONALE FOR MY INVESTIGATION" SECTION

While spreading across the country like politicians on a campaign trail, convenience stores appear to have maintained a fairly distinctive regional character. Uni-Mart and Sheetz are common names for these stores in central Pennsylvania, but in Iowa we find Casey's, in Massachusetts Cumberland Farms, and hundreds of other names specific to a state or region. . . . I am intrigued by the rapid growth of convenience stores, which, from my early research, seem to retain a local flavor for such a widespread national phenomenon.

EXCERPT FROM THE "PROCEDURE" SECTION

Through my library research, I will examine the burgeoning of convenience stores by exploring the answers to questions such as the following:

—How does the rapid growth of convenience stores reflect demographic trends?
—What (if anything) determines the location of convenience stores? (macro-geography?)
—How have the unrelated markets of food retail and gasoline sales evolved into a common store?

I also plan to interview several key executives at Uni-Mart, including Charles R. Markham who is the executive vice-president.

EXCERPT FROM THE "REFERENCES" SECTION

Directory of Supermarkets, Grocery, and Convenience Store Chains. CGS, 1990. This is a comprehensive guide to all major and many minor stores and their data (number of stores, size, brief history, top personnel). It also includes maps that illustrate regional concentrations of stores, and provides an overview of the industry today.

Curtis, C.E. "Mobil Wants To Be Your Milkman." *Forbes.* February 13, 1984, pp. 44-45. This article provides a concise but informative discussion of the combining of the food retail and gas industries.

Progress reports are common and highly important in science and engineering, typically when you are part of a research team reporting to a funding agency about your progress on work you are doing for that agency. The basic point of a progress report is to summarize the status, progress, and likely future for a particular project. In a progress report you are often expected to commit to an exact schedule for the project completion, discuss the status of the materials being used and account for the money spent, and summarize concretely both the

Progress Reports

current results and the predicted results. The professionalism of the progress report is often critical to the future of the project.

In writing-intensive courses, progress reports are used as a way for you to summarize your progress to your research advisor, who will typically give feedback on whether he or she is satisfied with your progress. These reports could feel like a huge waste of time to you, particularly if you have communicated with your advisor regularly about your work. However, progress reports are important professional documents, and they are an excellent opportunity to articulate some of the key sentences of your final report and even pose questions in writing to your advisor. The rules for writing progress reports are a lot more flexible in a writing-intensive course than they are on the job, with a lot less at stake, so you should take full advantage of the opportunity for practice.

Style for Progress Reports

- Include the working title of your report and the words "Progress Report" at the top of the page.

- Use section headings in the report to simplify both the writing and reading process.

- Open the report with a "Scope and Purpose" section, where you give a condensed version of your future report's introduction and objective.

- Always include a section entitled, for example, "Progress," which summarizes the work's pace and progress and explains any snafus, dilemmas, or set-backs.

- Always include a section entitled, for example, "Remaining Work," which honestly assesses the work that must still be completed. Think right on the page in this section, posing questions, speculating meaningfully, exploring your options.

- Always include a section that projects the expected results. Commit to a schedule for obtaining those results if possible.

- If necessary, include a section in which you directly solicit advice from your advisor. Be forthright and professional about the nature of the advice you need.

- Keep your paragraphs short and focused. Consider just one or two paragraphs per section as sufficient in most cases.

- Remember that your progress report is a one-on-one professional communication between you and your advisor, so your tone can often be straightforward and familiar. Therefore, as a rule, you can use "I" and "you" freely.

- Avoid statements that are overly optimistic, pessimistic, apologetic, cocky, or self-deprecating.

Sample Progress Report

The following excerpts from a progress report, written by a student in geosciences, provide an excellent example of how concrete and affirmative a progress report can be. Note the specificity even in the title, and how sections such as "Remaining Questions" and "Expected Results" demonstrate that the writer, even though he is two months away from the completion of his thesis, is thinking about the work in a professional manner.

PROGRESS REPORT
"Stratagraphic Architecture of Deep-Ramp Carbonates: Implications for Deposition of Volcanic Ashes, Salona and Coburn Formations, Central Pennsylvania"

by Andrew Hoover

EXCERPT FROM THE "SCOPE AND PURPOSE" SECTION:

The Late Middle Ordovician-age Salona and Coburn formations of central Pennsylvania show cyclic patterns on a decimeter scale and on a scale of tens of meters. . . . Little research has been done on sequence stratigraphy of deep-water mixed carbonate/siliciclastic systems, and a depositional model for this environment is necessary to understand the timing and processes of deposition. The stratigraphic position of the bentonites at the base of the larger cycles is significant because it indicates that they accumulated during a time of non-deposition in a deep water environment.

EXCERPT FROM THE "PROGRESS" SECTION

To date, I have described five lithofacies present in the Salona and Coburn formations. Two lithofacies are interpreted as storm deposits and make up the limestone component of the thinly-bedded couplets. . . . Some trends were observed in the raw data; however, because of the "noisy" nature of the data, a plot of the five-point moving average of bed thickness was created to define the cycles better.

EXCERPT FROM THE "ADDITIONAL WORK" SECTION

Two additional tasks are to be completed in the coming weeks. . . . With the results of these tests and the field observations, I will create a model for deposition of a deep-ramp mixed carbonate/siliciclastic system in a foreland basin environment. The model will include depositional processes, types of deposits, stratigraphic architecture, and tectonic setting.

EXCERPT FROM THE "REMAINING QUESTIONS" SECTION

Questions remain regarding the depositional processes responsible for the featureless micrite at the base of the Salona Formation. . . . How rapid was the transition? What record remains of the transition, if any? .

. . Were bentonites not deposited, or were they selectively removed at certain locations by erosive storm processes?

EXCERPT FROM THE "EXPECTED RESULTS" SECTION

In the coming months, I expect to find that the large-scale cycles represent parasequences. Flooding surfaces are marked by bentonites and shales, with bentonites removed in some locations. If the cycles are true parasequences, the implication is that eustatic sea level changes and not tectonic influences controlled the depositional changes over the interval.

Memos

In many writing-intensive courses, you are asked to submit your writing in memo form, and in some cases your assignments themselves are given to you as memos. This not only gives you practice in writing a professional document, it invites you to see your writing as purposeful and aimed at a particular audience. A detailed instructional memo about memo writing follows.

A Memo About Memo Writing

WRITING-INTENSIVE COURSES, INC.

memo

DATE: May 12, 1995
TO: Users of *Style for Students*
FROM: Joe Schall
SUBJECT: Writing Memos for your Classes

This memo provides you with tips on writing memos for your classes, with special attention to a memo's purpose, format, organization, content, tone, and style. Because my advice comes in the form of a memo, you can use this document as something of a model for your own work.

It is useful to begin by considering that a memo's purpose is to create an essentially one-on-one communication between writer and reader. Although a memo may be written to a group of people or with various audiences in mind, usually it is a highly goal-oriented communication between two people who need to share information. When you write a memo to a professor in the classroom setting, you are much like the employee who has been assigned to investigate a problem and report back to a supervisor. Therefore, you are expected to provide concrete information, even information that the supervisor might already know, in a form that clarifies ideas and puts them into context. Your fundamental job is to help the reader understand the most relevant issues.

The overall format of a memo can be broken down into the heading, the body, and the closing notations. What follows is a brief description of each:

- The *heading* has two parts: part one includes two centered lines at the top of page 1, identifying the name of the company or institution on the first line and the word "memo" on the second line; part two includes the four lines that you see at the top of this sample memo at the left margin (DATE, TO, etc.), filled in with the appropriate information. You may skip a single line between each of the four lines if you wish.

- The *body* of the memo is the text itself, which is usually presented in single-spaced paragraphs with a line skipped between each paragraph. The first lines of new paragraphs can appear at the left margin or they can be indented five spaces.

- The *closing notations,* which are used to identify such things as attachments, appear at the left margin two lines below the text of the final paragraph. By simply typing the word "Attachment" as a closing notation, you automatically refer the reader to any attachment, such as a map or References page, that is appended to your memo.

The overall organization of a memo mirrors, in most ways, that of an essay: an introduction, followed by body paragraphs, followed by a conclusion. However, the first paragraph of a memo is typically used as a forecasting device. Note how the opening paragraph of this memo defines the memo's function and reflects its organization. It is sensible to open memos for your classes in the same way, first directly stating the memo's purpose and establishing context and organization, then, perhaps in a new paragraph, beginning to provide the background in more detail. Paragraphs should not be too bulky—three or more per page is generally ideal. Finally, you should take full advantage of the same organizational tools that you use when you write an essay: meaningful topic sentences; carefully selected transition words; focused section headings; indented blocks to cite text or provide a series of examples; powerful punctuation marks such as the colon, semicolon, and dash.

A memo's content, of course, is guided by the assignment itself and the research required. It is important to remember as you present the content that selectivity and relevance matter greatly. Your job is to select the most relevant, most current information that is available to you, and to document the sources of your information just as you would in an essay. Do not, hesitate, of course, to let your memo's content be heavily informed by your research, but also provide your own interpretation and organization of this research wherever you can.

In business memos, the tone is often informal, but memos for your classes probably require a relatively formal, informative tone. Your basic goal is to pass on and interpret information in a savvy manner, so your tone must be no-nonsense and straightforward. At the same time, stylish prose is key to effective writing in science and engineering, and you should not hesitate to use active, interpretive adverbs and verbs and concrete, precise adjectives and nouns.

Finally, the closing paragraph of a memo should not provide a summary of the memo's entire contents, but a true conclusion—that is, a conviction or recommendation based on the evidence presented. The closing paragraph is the place to spell out the bottom line to the reader. Therefore, I close with my bottom line about writing memos for your classes: Use standard memo format to present your text; use internal organizational tools such as topic sentences, transition words, and powerful punctuation marks to enhance the flow of ideas, and write with the same clarity and concreteness expected of you in any essay.

Essays and Term Papers

When you are first faced with writing a long essay or term paper it can be intimidating, but you can make your job and the reader's job easier by following the general advice that follows. Of course, if your professors offer you any specific guidelines about paper writing be sure to follow them first. Otherwise, incorporate the advice that follows into your papers wherever appropriate.

Mechanics

Of course, papers should always be typed if possible, double-spaced on 8-1/2 x 11 paper on one side of the page only, and letter-quality print or better is always expected. Often you are expected to supply a cover sheet giving the date, your name, the title of the paper, the class, and the professor's name. Tables and figures should be numbered consecutively throughout the text, and if there are a good number of them, then separate lists of tables and figures at the beginning of the paper may be expected. Tables and figures should always have descriptive captions, and if they come directly from sources, the sources must be specifically credited in the captions with the same citation style that you used throughout the paper.

Title

Many writers do not settle on a final title until the paper is completed, but choosing a working title as you compose will certainly help you to focus. The final title should be succinct and definitive, individual and informational. Clearly, the title "An Overview of the Hydraulic Fracturing of Methane-Bearing Coal Formations" is more complete, satisfying, and accurate than "Hydraulic Fracturing." The title is important because it announces the paper's specific content and often serves as a pathway to the paper's thesis.

Introduction

Your Introduction is your opportunity to be at your most individual. You should get your reader's attention immediately by precisely announcing the paper's subject or by launching into a relevant scenario or narrative that informs or illustrates your overall argument. A paper illustrating the costly effects of poor mine design, for instance, might open with the scenario of how a poorly designed pillar at a salt mine in Louisiana once collapsed, fracturing the surface above and draining an entire lake into the mine. A paper on the supply and demand of nickel might begin by straightforwardly announcing that the paper will explain the uses of nickel, detail its market structure, and use data to forecast the future supply and demand of the metal.

In brief, a paper's introduction should define and limit the paper's scope and purpose, indicate some sense of organization, and, whenever possible, suggest an overall argument. Another good rule of thumb is that the introduction should be problem-focused, giving the reader enough background so that the paper's importance and relationship to key ideas are clear.

As examples of how creative an introduction can be, here are the opening lines from a geography paper and a paper on optics, both of which use narrative technique to arouse our interest. Note how the first excerpt uses an "I" narrator comfortably while the second excerpt does not use "I" even though the writer is clearly thoughtful. The first excerpt is from a paper on the genericism of America's highway exit ramp services and the second is from a paper on shape constancy.

> The observation struck me slowly, a growing sense of déjà vu. I was driving the endless miles of Interstate 70 crossing Kansas when I began to notice that the exits all looked the same. . . .

> Our eyes often receive pictures of the world that are contrary to physical reality. A pencil in a glass of water miraculously bends; railroad tracks converge in the distance. . . .

Thesis Statement / Objective

Most papers have outright thesis statements or objectives. Normally you will not devote a separate section of the paper to this; in fact, often the thesis or objective is conveniently located either right at the beginning or right at the end of the Introduction. A good thesis statement fits only the paper in which it appears. Thesis statements usually forecast the paper's content, present the paper's fundamental hypothesis, or even suggest that the paper is an argument for a particular way of thinking about a topic. Avoid the purely mechanical act of writing things like "The first topic covered in this paper is x. The second topic covered is y. The third topic is . . ." Instead, concretely announce the most important elements of your topic and suggest your fundamental approach—even point us toward the paper's conclusion if you can.

Here are two carefully focused and precisely worded thesis statements, both of which appeared at the ends of introductory paragraphs:

> This paper reviews the problem of Pennsylvania's dwindling landfill space, evaluates the success of recycling as a solution to this problem, and challenges the assumption that Pennsylvania will run out of landfill space by the year 2000.

> As this paper will show, the fundamental problem behind the Arab-Israeli conflict is the lack of a workable solution to the third stage of partition, which greatly hinders the current negotiations for peace.

Body Paragraphs / Section Headings

Never simply label the middle bulk of the paper as "Body" and then lump a bunch of information into one big section. Instead, organize the body of your paper into sections by using an overarching principle that supports your thesis, even if that simply means presenting four different methods for solving some problem one method at a time. Normally you are allowed and encouraged to use section headings to help both yourself and the reader follow the flow of the paper. Always word your section headings clearly, and do not stray from the subject that you have identified within a section.

As examples, I offer you two sets of section headings taken from essays. The first is from Dr. Craig Bohren's "Understanding Colors in Nature" (1), which appeared in a 1990 edition of Earth & Mineral Sciences; the second is from an economics paper on the supply and demand of asbestos.

Section Headings From "Understanding Colors In Nature"
Color By Scattering: The Role of Particle Size
Color By Scattering: The Positions of Source and Observer
The Blue Sky: The Role of Multiple Scattering
Color By Absorption in Multiple-Scattering Media
Color by Absorption: Microscopic Mechanisms are Sometimes
  Elusive

Section Headings From "Asbestos: Its Supply and Demand"
Industry Structure
The Mining and Properties of Asbestos
World Resources and Reserves
Byproducts and Co-products
Economic Factors and Supply and Demand Problems
Uses of and Substitutes for Asbestos
The Issue of Health on Supply and Demand

Just by considering the section headings in the above examples, we can begin to see the fundamental structures and directions of the essays, because both sets of headings break the paper topic into its natural parts and suggest some sort of a moving forward through a topic. Note how these headings—as all section headings should—tell us the story of the paper and are worded just as precisely as any title should be.

Most importantly then, you must use your section headings in the same way that you use topic sentences or thesis statements: to control, limit, and organize your own thinking for your reader's sake.

Conclusion

Most papers use "Conclusion" as a heading for the final section of the text, although there are times when headings such as "Future

Trends" will serve equally well for a paper's closing section. When you are stuck for a conclusion, look back at your introduction; see if you can freshly reemphasize your objectives by outlining how they were met, or even revisit an opening scenario from the introduction in a new light to illustrate how the paper has brought about change. Your conclusion should not be a summary of the paper or a simple tacked-on ending, but a significant and logical realization of the paper's goals. Beware of the temptation to open your final paragraph with "In conclusion," or "In summary," and then summarize the paper. Instead, let your entire conclusion stand as a graceful termination of an argument. As you write your conclusion, concentrate on presenting the bottom line, and think of the word's definition: a conclusion is an articulated conviction arrived at on the basis of the evidence you have presented.

What follows is an excerpt from a conclusion to a paper entitled "Exercise in the Prevention and Treatment of Osteoporosis in Women." Note how it reflects directly on the paper's hypothesis and concretely spells out the bottom line, gracefully bringing closure to the paper's argument:

> The majority of evidence presented in this paper supports the hypothesis that exercise positively affects bone mineral density in both premenopausal and postmenopausal women. Exercise has been shown to increase bone mineral density in premenopausal women even after the teenage years, and it preserves the bone mass achieved in the following decades. There is also evidence that exercise adds a modest, yet significant amount of bone mass to the postmenopausal skeleton. As these findings demonstrate, women of all ages can benefit by regular weight-bearing exercise, an increased intake of calcium-rich foods, and—for postmenopausal women—the maintenance of adequate estrogen levels. It is never too late to prevent osteoporosis or lessen its severity by making appropriate lifestyle choices.

References

Any sources cited must be correctly listed on a References page using the Author-Year or Number system (see Chapter 6 of this manual).

For those of you in such technical fields as ceramic science, metallurgy, nuclear engineering, or electrical engineering, you might find the reading of journal articles none too stimulating (other than the occasional exciting references to hot presses, cool gels, quickened pulses, or body melds). Nevertheless, at their best, the journal articles you must read are certainly important and carefully crafted. The rigid-seeming format and objective style of scientific reports lend a universality to them so that various kinds of readers can readily access and use the complex information. Your professors will confirm that scientists rarely read these reports linearly—many readers cut

Technical Reports

right to "Results and Discussion" or look over the tables and figures before reading anything, then jump around to those bits of the report that are most relevant to their individual needs.

In light of the above realities, it is especially important for you to write reports in a fashion acceptable to a journal in your field. As you prepare technical reports for your writing-intensive courses, you have built-in slots in which to put your information, and you plug in to a tried and proven recipe that has evolved over many years. Understanding this recipe and conforming to it will help you to organize your complex information as well as meet your reader's specific and sophisticated needs. For a more intensive and much fatter look at this recipe from an editor's point of view, check out "The Universal Recipe For Scientific Reports," reprinted in Chapter 9 of this manual. In briefer form, what follows are guidelines that you can apply as you prepare technical reports for your classes.

Mechanics

Of course, reports should always be typed, double-spaced on 8-1/2 x 11 paper on one side of the page only, and letter-quality print or better is expected. Unless you are instructed otherwise, it is usually standard to include a cover sheet giving the date, your name, the title of the paper, the course, and the professor's name. Tables and figures should be numbered consecutively throughout the text, and, in a thesis or long report, separate lists of tables and figures are normally included at the beginning of the paper. Tables and figures should always have descriptive captions, and if they come directly from sources then the sources must be properly credited in the captions. Never present tables and figures without some useful interpretation of them in the text.

Title

It is always necessary to have a highly concrete title consisting only of words that contribute directly to the paper's subject. Be sure that the title contains no filler and includes few abbreviations or acronyms, yet also be certain that it is complete. "Sol Gel Method" is clearly incomplete compared to "The Synthesis of NZP by the Sol Gel Method," while "The Role of Solid Oxide Fuel Cells in the Search For Energy Alternatives as Necessitated by the Recent Middle East Crisis" is excessive and should be reduced to its essential elements.

Abstract

Most reports require an Abstract—a condensed summary of the report's contents. In a journal article, more people will read the abstract than any other part of the paper, so its succinctness and accuracy are vital. The abstract is always self-contained, and is sometimes presented as a separate page. The best abstracts do these things:

- summarize the specific nature of the investigation.

- identify the rationale behind the investigation.

- present the important findings and most significant overall data.

- briefly interpret the pertinent findings.

By necessity, abstracts are often written last, and a good rule of thumb is that the abstract is less than 5 percent of the paper's total length. In a thesis, an abstract should always fit on one page if possible. Passive voice and past tense verbs are appropriate for the purposes of summary. What follows is a short excerpt from the opening of an abstract:

> The formation of a manganese-metallized layer on the surface of silicon-nitrate ceramics by the vapor diffusion method was studied. Pure manganese powder was used as a vapor source. The metallization was carried out by…

Introduction

The Introduction should offer immediate context for the reader by establishing why the problem being studied is important and by describing the nature and scope of the problem. You should describe your particular approach to some problem and establish how your investigative work meshes with the specific needs of the field or with other work that has been done. The funnel system—moving from a broad approach to a gradually narrowed scope—is highly recommended here. Present tense is also highly favored, especially as you present scientific truths and the objectives of the report. Introductions range from one to several pages, and must always include a clearly worded account of the report's objective, usually at the exact end of the introduction (Some writers even include a short separate section labeled "Objective"). Most journals allow "we" or "our" to be used once or twice in the introduction, especially as you outline your objectives or summarize the common goals of researchers. Here is an ideal opening sentence from an introduction; note how it launches the reader directly into the science:

> In order to produce highly reliable metal-ceramic joints, we must fully understand the joining mechanisms.

Literature Review

When articles appear in journals, the most noteworthy literature will usually be reviewed only briefly in the Introduction or as it becomes relevant. In technical reports for your classes, however, an entire section of your paper may well be devoted to a Literature Review. Literature reviews range from exhaustive searches to summaries of only the most germane articles, but the fundamental objective is always the same: to establish the history of the problem being investigated by summarizing the WHAT, HOW, and WHY of the work that has already been done. Writing a literature review often requires you to establish relationships among experiments and to condense a dozen or so pages of published material into one short original paragraph. Passive voice may seem tempting to use, but simple past tense and active voice will serve you well here, because you can smoothly place the author's name(s) into the subject slot of the sentence:

> Yoldas and Lloyd proposed a chemical polymerization technique for the preparation of NASICON gels.

Naturally, you must cite the literature appropriately as you summarize it. Rely on present tense to state scientific truths and past tense to summarize the findings of other authors.

Experimental / Methods / Procedures

Any of the above titles will usually do for this section, although journals and professors will certainly have particular preferences. The goal is to summarize the WHAT, HOW, and WHY behind your specific experiment, with particular emphasis on the WHAT and HOW so that other researchers can repeat your procedures if they so desire. As necessary, this section includes a description of the relevant apparatus and materials used, and photographs and diagrams could be used sparingly to help clarify the procedures. Passive voice and past tense verbs are essential in this section, but be sure that your sentences are written efficiently and contain simple subjects and verbs when possible. Here is an ideal sentence from the "Experimental" section of an engineering report:

> After the dispersion thickened it was poured into molds coated with Vaseline to prevent sticking.

This basic format of directly saying "what was done, why it was done" should be used over and over in the "Experimental" section.

Finally, subsections, perhaps numbered, may be used to aid in the organization of the material. For example:

```
2.0 EXPERIMENTAL
    2.1 Apparatus
            2.1.1 Heat treatment furnace
            2.1.2 Tensile testing device
    2.2 Materials
```

Results

For most readers, this is the most important section of the report, because your readers must easily find your data in order to interpret it. Here is where you straightforwardly present the results of your experiment, usually with minimal interpretation or discussion. Naturally, the use of tables, graphs, and figures is especially enlightening here, as are explanations of just how the data were derived:

> The conductivities of the top and bottom values for each measurement were averaged and the results are listed in Table 3.

Take care not to include your experimental methods themselves here—that is the job of the previous section.

Discussion

Often this section is combined with "Results" into one "Results and Discussion" section; this allows you to interpret your results as you summarize them. Logical deductions must be made, errors of or ambiguities in the data should be discussed, and causal relationships must be confirmed. It is important here not to rely on a table or figure to do the work for you—you must truly and concisely interpret. Beware of making sweeping generalizations or unfounded statements. Again, passive voice may seem tempting here, but active voice can be highly valuable, especially as you make a logical assertion:

> Obviously, the protective oxide layer formed to prevent rapid oxidation.

As a rule, use past tense to summarize your actual results; use present tense to present established facts or present your interpretations ("The helium sintering data show . . .").

Conclusions

In "Discussion" you supplied your reasoning; now you present the precise conclusions you have arrived at as they relate to your experimental objectives. Conclusions may be listed and numbered, and there should be a sense of how they contribute to the understanding of the overall problem. In a sense, you are going back to the big picture provided by your introduction now, but, unless you are instructed otherwise, do not summarize your introduction all over again; instead, incorporate your conclusions into the big picture, even suggesting where more work is needed. This section may be short—often about the same length as the abstract. The following is an excerpt from the "Conclusions" section of a report:

> These results confirm the hypothesis posed in the Introduction: that the shock sensitivity of this explosive is probably not due to the weakening of the phenyl ring by the substituents. It is possible, however, that

mechanical properties such as the coefficient of friction, uniaxial yield stress, and hardness greatly influence the explosive's shock sensitivity. Further work is needed in this area to determine…

Acknowledgments

If appropriate, briefly recognize any individual or institution that contributed directly to the completion of the research through financial support, technical assistance, or critique. In a thesis, this section may appear just before the introduction.

References

All sources cited must be correctly listed on a References page using the Author–Year or Number system (see Chapter 6 of this manual).

Appendices

If necessary, use an "Appendices" section to present supplementary material that was not included in the main body of the paper because it would have detracted in some way from the efficient or logical presentation of the text, usually either by sheer bulk or level of relevance. A typical appendix would be a list of organizations relevant to the material of the report, or a list of symbols used in the text, or the derivation of an equation that was used in the text but could not be referenced because it did not originally appear in a standard text. As with figures and tables, appendices should be numbered or lettered in sequence; i.e., "Appendix A, Appendix B," and so on.

Oral Reports

Especially in the academic or corporate world, excellent oral presentation skills are vital. Those scientists and engineers who can communicate on their feet, as well as in writing, are highly valued by their colleagues and superiors. Oral presentation skills are so important to professional organizations that they usually provide members with their preferred guidelines for presenting papers at small meetings or symposia. For instance, the Society For Mining, Metallurgy, And Exploration, Inc. distributes a fourteen-page guide on "How To Prepare Your Meeting Paper," which includes everything from metric conversion tables to the suggestion that you avoid a monotone as you speak at a meeting. Some organizations even give their views on such things as ideal titles for talks or the pitfalls of bad body language. It is wise, even if you are just beginning to think about one day presenting a professional talk, to write to any professional organizations in your field and ask for oral presentation guidelines (as well as style manuals, which some organizations also provide free of charge). These guidelines give you an inside look at how professionals conduct themselves, and it is never too early to be thinking about how others in your field communicate successfully with each other.

The most important thing for a speaker to realize while giving a talk is that the audience's needs are the first and best touchstone for deciding how to present information. A speaker, of course, has an agenda in mind when giving a talk, but this should be on the back burner; what matters most is who the principal audience members are and what is most advantageous for them to hear. If the principal audience is management, for instance, finances and utility might well be the focus; if the audience is other engineers who are the speaker's peers, the presentation might emphasize equations, calculations, and models.

As a capstone to a writing-intensive course, especially a senior thesis course, you will often be asked to give an oral presentation of your work as well as a written one. The talk's goal is not usually to represent the totality of your research, but to inform an audience about a topic meaningful to them. As you prepare and give any oral presentation, keep the following tips in mind:

Preparation and General Presentation

- A talk is not the format for reading a paper. In fact, talks are often mere warm-ups for a paper that is later published. Never simply read from a paper, but do not be afraid to consult carefully prepared (clearly handwritten or even typed) notecards.

- Use an introduction at the beginning of your talk and a summary afterwards to highlight your major points. Some speakers even offer a concise written summary with bulleted points on a transparency or handout to ensure followability.

- Practice your talk straight through, and as you go jot quick notes to yourself about how to improve it. If you can not manage to practice your talk straight through, maybe you are not yet ready to give it.

- Ideally, practice your talk under conditions similar to those in which you will give it, considering such factors as acoustics, distance from the audience, and room size. Be mentally prepared to adapt to the appropriate conditions.

- Only invite discussion if the format and time allow it, and, in general, only take questions at the end so that you are not sidetracked.

- Choose an appropriately snappy title. You are expected not to come off as stodgy. Which talk would you rather attend: "And On The Eighth Day, God Created Fractals," or "Fractals—Specific Geometrical Objects with Fractional Dimensions—And Their Various Applications to Nature in General and The Universe At Large"?

- When you give a talk professionally, always request guidelines for talks from any relevant organizations and conform to them explicitly. It would be embarrassing for you if you were expected to present units in metric, for example, and you did otherwise because you failed to request or follow the available guidelines.

Visual Aids

- Consider the use of some simple, meaningful props; even pass them around. Props keep your audience interested and, especially if they represent the actual work you did, they underscore the nature of that work.

- Take care not to stand in the way of your visual aids.

- Do not hesitate to use a chalkboard or easel. They are especially good for writing down basic information that you also want your audience to write down, or for presenting a picture as it evolves via its individual pieces (e.g., a flow chart, schematic, or experimental set-up).

- Keep visual aids as simple and uncluttered as possible, and if the information must be complex, prioritize it for your audience as you present it (e.g., if presenting a ten-column table, direct your audience to the most significant columns).

- View all of your visuals from your audience's perspective prior to your talk. Be sure that your audience can easily see all that you want them to see.

- A rule of thumb is that you offer only one major point per illustration. If you need to focus on more than one point, re-present the illustration in another form on a separate visual with the different point emphasized.

- As a rule, point to the projected image of your visual (use a pointer or light pen if possible) rather than the original source. For example, point to the screen rather than the transparency itself on the overhead projector.

- Plan and present visuals so that their longest dimension is horizontal rather than vertical. Use both uppercase and lowercase letters and orient pictures from left to right.

- When you are not using a visual, keep it out of sight or out of your audience's line of attention. Turn off the light on overhead projectors when no visuals are relevant; actually invite your audience to turn their attention away from an easel or chalkboard when appropriate.

Your Manner As You Speak

- Maintain eye contact with at least a few people—especially those who are being the most responsive—in various parts of the room.

- Speak in short sentences and think in short paragraphs so that your listeners can easily follow you.

- Refer to time as an organizational tool: "For the next two minutes, I will summarize the current uses of computerized tomography, then I will move on to . . . "

- Do not be afraid to pause occasionally to give your listeners time to digest your information and give yourself a moment for reorientation.

- Avoid talking sideways or backwards at your audience. Pause when you have to turn or point to something, then turn back towards the audience, then talk.

- Use physical gestures sparingly and with intention. For instance, raise three fingers and say "thirdly" as you make your third point; pull your hands toward your chest slightly as you advocate the acceptance of an idea. Beware, though, of overusing your body, especially idiosyncratically.

- Pronounce all words correctly, especially those key to the discipline. Check pronunciation of ambiguous words beforehand to be certain. It would be embarrassing to mispronounce "Euclidian" or "Möbius strip" or "sciatic" in front of a group of people that you want to impress.

- Keep your feet firmly rooted and avoid continual shuffling of your weight. Intentionally leaning slightly on one leg most of the time can keep you comfortable and relaxed.

- Avoid clichés, slang, colloquialisms, and overformality. Instead use visual language, concrete nouns, active single-word verbs.

- Be animated, but carefully so—many notches above Joe Friday, but many notches below Pee Wee Herman.

Improving Your Style

*In composing, as a general rule, run your pen
through every other word you have written; you have
no idea what vigour it will give your style.*
                                    —Sydney Smith

Suppose you have never been told or have never believed that you
are a good writer, and you seriously doubt that you can improve
your style. Or suppose you have a draft ready but you or another
reader you trust just plain does not find it highly readable or interesting, and you know you have got to make it livelier somehow. Or suppose you are tempted to fall back on the idea that grades given to
papers are purely subjective, having little foundation in anything but
your picky old professor's pet peeves. If you find yourself huddling
anywhere underneath this umbrella, then this chapter is for you.

Everyone agrees that there has to be some level of subjectivity
when it comes to paper grading, but this subjectivity is guided by
instinct, professional experience, and concern for accuracy rather than
by whim. The frustrated professor who writes "Get your commas
right!" or "Where is your grammar?" is clearly commenting on non-
subjective grammatical problems in your paper, but that same professor may also write "Unclear" or "I can't follow this" or "Punch up
your verbs" on your paper—an indication that style is more than
grammar, and that, as a representative, thinking reader, your professor
believes that you must write better.

This chapter is devoted to helping you improve your style. You
will find discussion of the basics of grammar, topic sentences, and
paragraphs, word lists that give you the tools to improve your style,
and short lessons on the stylistic conventions of science and engineering. In a nutshell, this chapter will help you to revise your work—the
key to improving your style.

Professors who care about writing will always make a strong
plea for Concision, Precision, and Revision (CPR). After college, the probability that what you write will be read is inversely pro-
portional to its length and comprehensibility. In college, even though
your professors have to read your papers, you should apply CPR to
whatever you write to reap maximum benefits. In other words, you
should use words concisely and precisely, and you should make a
habit of revising your writing. Some advice from *The Elements of Style*
(1), by Strunk and White, drives the point home beautifully:

Concision, Precision, Revision

Chapter 2

- A sentence should contain no unnecessary words, a paragraph no unnecessary sentences, for the same reason that a drawing should have no unnecessary lines and a machine no unnecessary parts.

This sentence is important because it affirms the message that writing has utility—it performs work. Many scientists and engineers have memorized this sentence and consciously apply it to their writing. You should too.

With the advice from Strunk and White in mind, read the poorly written paragraph that follows:

Increasing foreign competition and technological change, in a variety of forms, are, as they always have been, disrupting various well-established patterns in terms of industrial organization. An apparent growing quality in the upward movement of economic change is also causing geographers' interest in regional adjustment problems to grow as well: problems that often focus concern on regional economic decline in a context of low rates of national productivity improvement on loss of international competitiveness in sectors such as automobiles and primary metals.

You *can* sort out the meaning of this paragraph if you work hard enough, but why bother? The paragraph just does not seem to be designed to communicate its message clearly. But let us improve this paragraph with the goal of concision, precision, and revision. We can begin by cutting the needless and virtually meaningless words from the first few sentences—words such as "in a variety of forms," "various," and "in terms of." Next, more precision can be created in those words that are the least precise—for example, "an apparent growing quality"—and the long and unfathomable last sentence of the paragraph should be cut up into its natural pieces. Clearer connections among sentences could also be supplied via simple, standard transition words.

Here is a revised version of the paragraph after CPR.

Recently, increasing foreign competition and technological change have disrupted well-established patterns of industrial organization. This acceleration in economic change has heightened geographers' interest in regional adjustment problems, drawing attention to regional economic decline in such sectors as automobiles and primary metals. Regional economic decline often manifests itself through low rates of national productivity improvement and a loss of international competitiveness.

Perhaps this is not the best version of this paragraph, but certainly it is much better than the original. Now the paragraph's true topic (regional economic decline) is much clearer, and each sentence is clearly designed to relate to the sentence next to it. In a word, the paragraph is now tidy; before revision, it was a mess.

Finally, I urge you to buy *The Elements of Style,* by Strunk and White. It is cheap, easy to use, and can be read in just a few hours. It is available in almost any bookstore for about three bucks. Scientists and engineers recommend it and use it, because it covers all of the nuts and bolts of good writing in a concise and precise way. Spend a few dollars and get to know Strunk and White. Your readers will be grateful.

Subject/Verb Agreement

As you already know, you have to be sure that paired subjects and verbs go together grammatically. What this usually means (especially when you write in present tense) is that if a subject is singular its accompanying verb gets an "s" added to it, but if the subject is plural the verb requires no "s" (i.e., "the material ages" and "the materials age" are both correct). Simple, right? Your ear confirms the subject/verb agreement for you. For most writers, though, confusion arises when the subject and verb are distanced from each other in the sentence. Consider this example:

The material applied to the blades of wind turbines age rapidly in tests.

Do you see the problem? The word "age" should be "ages" in order to be compatible with the sentence's subject—"the material"—but since "age" is right next to the plural "turbines" it is easy to get the grammar wrong.

The trick to subject/verb agreement is always to dissect the sentence mentally to determine which noun or pronoun goes with which verb. You can not always trust your ear, especially when the word you are using is a word such as "everybody," "everyone," or "one" (all of which are singular). Also, even though "United States" or "NASA" might sound to you as though it is plural, the United States is considered to be one country, and NASA (like other organizations or corporations) is one entity (i.e., "NASA redesigned its o-rings" is correct while "NASA redesigned their o-rings" is not). In contrast, a sentence subject that includes an "and" as part of the subject (e.g., "Rising productivity and profit . . .") is automatically a plural subject, and therefore a verb that goes with a plural subject (e.g., "are," "reveal") must be chosen.

Determining the correct grammar is often a matter of mentally breaking a sentence into its parts and considering how the words are related to each other, especially the key words that are part of the subject and verb.

A simple way to check whether your subjects and verbs are compatible is to supply a mental "they" for a plural subject and a mental "it" for a singular subject. (Grammatically, the phrase "The speed of the downdrafts was intense" is the same as "It was intense"; the phrase "Two of the variables are incorrect" is the same as "They are incorrect"). The longer or more complex your sentences are, the more likely you are to have to test out your subject/verb agreement at times.

Especially if you find that you are having consistent subject/verb agreement problems, you simply must make it a habit to do the following:

- Identify the subjects and verbs of your sentences, putting aside the other elements of the sentence momentarily.

- Test the subjects and verbs for compatibility, if necessary by mentally supplying "they" for plural subjects and "it" for singular subjects.

- Remember that a sentence subject that includes an "and" is a plural and will therefore need a verb that agrees with a plural.

- Remember that the names of organizations and words such as "everyone," anyone," "each"—i.e., words that ask us to consider something one member at a time—are singular.

- If the meaning or grammar of the sentence is unclear, consider revising so that the subject and verb are closer together in the sentence.

Tricky Singular/ Plural Pairs

What follows are some important and commonly misused singular/plural pairs, most of which you will probably be using regularly in your writing. In each case the singular is given first:

Singular	Plural
alga	algae
appendix	appendixes or appendices
axis	axes
crisis	crises
criterion	criteria
curriculum	curriculums or curricula
datum	data ("data" is commonly used as either singular or plural these days, but the plural is preferred by most writers)
formula	formulas or formulae
fungus	fungi
hypothesis	hypotheses
locus	loci
medium	media
nucleus	nuclei

Singular	Plural
phenomenon	phenomena
radius	radii
retina	retinas or retinae
spectrum	spectra
stimulus	stimuli
stratum	strata
thesis	theses

It is important, of course, to use the correct form of these nouns and to be certain that the related verbs are compatible with the fact that the noun is singular or plural. Even though they may automatically sound wrong to your ear, the sentences below are all correct, with the subjects and verbs compatible in grammar.

The data are both significant and surprising.

The emission spectra of the bodies peak in the infrared.

A stratum of sand was struck as they dug the well.

Droplets of different radii evaporate at different rates.

Verb Tense

Especially for those of you in highly technical fields, where you typically write scientific reports and coordinate your own research findings with those of other researchers, decisions about the proper verb tense to use in a given situation can be especially befuddling. The first rule of thumb is to word your sentences in such a way that verb tenses are as simple and consistent as possible. The easiest way to simplify things for both yourself and your reader is to use present tense when possible because it is automatically reader-friendly. But there is obviously more to it than that. Read on:

An accepted rule is that *scientific truths, general facts,* and *things happening during the reading of the paper* can be treated best in PRESENT TENSE.

Nickel is generally deposited from sulfate, sulfate-chloride, or sulfamate electrolytes with or without additives.

This paper evaluates material deformation in the brittle and ductile regimes.

Your *own findings* or *experimental procedures,* the actual *experimental procedures and results of others,* and *physically past events* should usually be treated as simple PAST TENSE (i.e., avoid using "had").

A drop of HNO_3 was added to bring the distilled water to pH 3.

In the 1930s, it was fashionable for scientists to write memos only in the passive voice.

FUTURE TENSE is usually reserved for those things that really are *not yet completed.* This tense is most useful when you want to talk about future events.

Copper use will become more sophisticated as new exploration technologies and new extraction techniques develop.

Finally, the PERFECT TENSE (using "has," "have," or "had" as a helping verb) is less frequently used, but it comes in handy when you are writing about a "double time"—that is, when you need to stress that *one thing happened before another,* or that *something began in the past and was continued thereafter.*

This particular radiometer has been used since 1985.

Scientists had argued about the existence of molecules for centuries before it was universally agreed that matter was discrete rather than continuous.

What Makes A Paragraph Tick?

There is no mystery about what makes good paragraphs: orderliness, coherence, completeness, and unity. Stylistically, these four attributes are usually accomplished by concrete topic sentences and smooth logical connections among ideas. Within paragraphs, writers usually connect ideas, thereby creating coherence and orderliness, by using combinations of the four methods described below. Capital letters indicate the words that help to establish the exact connections.

Four Methods For Writing Good Paragraphs

- Link the subjects of juxtaposed sentences.

    To heat the sample, TUNGSTEN-HALOGEN LAMPS are used below and above the fused silica tube. THESE LAMPS contain a tungsten filament and bromide gas inside a quartz bulb. By resistive heating alone, THE LAMPS can attain temperatures of 300° C to 400° C.

- Link the end of one sentence to the beginning of the next sentence.

    The film is not completely oriented in a single direction, and the system includes a number of ENTANGLEMENTS. THESE ENTANGLEMENTS become frozen into position as the film crystallizes.

- Link sentences through implicit similarity, repetition, contrast, or causality.

    When A SUBJECT VIEWS an object initially as a CIRCLE, that image becomes imprinted ON THE BRAIN. Even when the EYE AND BRAIN can distinguish an ellipse from the CIRCLE, memory tricks THE SUBJECT into seeing A CIRCLE.

The addition of oxygen promotes soot formation, particularly at low temperatures. ON THE OTHER HAND, oxygen also removes aromatic rings and active intermediates by oxidation, thus suppressing soot formation at high oxygen concentrations.

BECAUSE the wire is flexible, the sonde can rely on its own weight to pull it down the hole, essentially doing a free fall. THEREFORE, the sonde tends to get stuck easily in highly deviated holes.

- Establish a particular order and then follow through with that order.

Norris describes THREE FORMS of exit morphology. In the FIRST FORM, development has spread to both sides of the intersecting road but is still limited to one side of the interstate. In the SECOND FORM, development exists on both sides of the highway, and in the THIRD FORM, which Norris labels full development, services are located along both sides of the intersecting roads and along ancillary feeder roads.

Of course there are other ways of linking sentences, such as by time, and the above methods are not meant to suggest that writing a good paragraph is a purely mechanical act—a matter of just plugging in transition words or giving juxtaposed sentences similar subjects. But the fact is that good paragraphs tend to rely on the four methods listed above most of the time. As you write and revise your paragraphs, especially when you sense that flow is needed, look for opportunities to exploit the above methods properly and you will be improving your writing.

Topic Sentences

Most paragraphs need to have topic sentences. It is important to remember that topic sentences come in many forms and need not be the first sentences in paragraphs. However, if you have a paragraph that must be tidied up or you are composing a paragraph from scratch, writing a clear topic sentence as an opening statement is a good way to start.

In technical writing, topic sentences take a number of forms. They often simply *provide a general statement* for the paragraph to support:

The role of coal in the hydrology of strip mines receives little attention in the literature. Most groundwater analyses of potential or current strip mines are simply concerned with…

Often topic sentences simply *kick off a list of examples:*

There are obvious advantages associated with the real-time information that a measurement-while-drilling system supplies. The first advantage is…

Other topic sentences *supply background or announce scenarios:*

Ceramic tubes are now being used in the most aggressive environments. In industry…

Some topic sentences *combine the listing of examples and background material:*

Three points about the geologic activity of wind and the development of landscapes in dry lands are relevant here. First…

It is clear that a simple, straightforward topic sentence is usually the best way to introduce general background, examples, scenarios, arguments, or even to establish a direct linkage to the preceding paragraph. The fundamental thing to realize is that good writers use concrete and efficient topic sentences to *control* and *unify* their paragraphs. If you use the topic sentence as a tool to organize your thoughts, your paragraph content will fall into place more readily.

Transition Words

What follows is a handy list of common transition words and their functions. If you open sentences appropriately with these words it will help your writing to flow. Always keep the literal meaning of a transition word in mind as you use it—therefore, do not use "for example" unless you truly are introducing an example that links to the preceding information; do not use "nevertheless" unless you truly are offering a contrasting point. Note how this paragraph has required a minimal use of transition words; they should not be forced in where they do not belong. When you do use them, keep their broader functions (i.e., "contrast," "emphasis," etc.) directly in mind.

Causality
Accordingly
Consequently
For this reason
Hence
Therefore
Thus

Intention
For this purpose
In order to do this
To this end
With this in mind

Location
Beyond
Here
Nearby
Opposite
Overlying (underlying)
There
To the right (left)

Emphasis
Above all
Certainly
Clearly
Indeed
In fact
In short
Obviously
Of course

Closure
In conclusion
In sum
On the whole
To summarize

Interpretation
Fortunately
Interestingly
Significantly
Surprisingly

Amplification
Again
Also
Apparently
Besides
Equally important
Finally
First, Second, etc.
Further
In addition
Moreover

Detail
Especially
In particular
Namely
Specifically
To enumerate

Similarity
Likewise
Similarly

Time	Contrast	Concession
Afterward	However	At any rate
At the same time	In contrast	At least
Before	Nevertheless	
Earlier	On the contrary	
In the meantime	On the other hand	
Sometimes	Still	
Later		
Next	**Example**	
Preceding this	For example	
Simultaneously	For instance	
Soon	To illustrate	
Until		

Using Active Verbs

Because of the nature of what you write and read, it is natural for you to feel enticed by generic all-purpose verbs such as "deal with" or "show," which on the surface can sound snappy and technical. Even in journal articles, these verbs put in a shocking number of appearances and return for many unsolicited encores. Yet these words convey no analytical meaning at all and are barely informational. Much to the reader's frustration, "deal with" and "show" are merely thinly disguised excuses for much more active analytical verbs such as *theorize, suggest, imply, propose*. For the reader, "Cheswick dealt with" or "Figure 4 shows" are far less meaningful than "Cheswick hypothesized" or "Figure 4 represents." As always, you should choose exact words in favor of nonspecific ones, especially when you can use an active verb.

What follows is a substantial list of active verbs. Each of these words is packed with individual, analytical meaning. This list is especially meaningful for you as you prepare a *Literature Review* or *describe your own work*—say, in a *thesis statement*. As always, be sure to choose the best verb for the situation—verbs such as "construct," "challenge," and "extrapolate" are completely different from each other, so you must use them with meaningful care.

Active Verbs That Describe Work

yield	illustrate	illuminate	reveal	employ
mean	suggest	clarify	indicate	represent
prove	insist	propose	imply	assert
postulate	consider	infer	state	extrapolate
estimate	define	classify	invoke	analyze
compare	hypothesize	synthesize	summarize	disagree
generalize	narrate	evaluate	simplify	measure
note	predict	introduce	report	challenge
delineate	depict	construe	interpret	provide
acknowledge	distinguish	inform	specify	restrict
determine	detail	sum up	designate	point out

Active Verbs That Describe Work (continued)

set forth	deduce	derive	characterize	guide
maintain	believe	speculate	present	organize
investigate	assess	determine	calculate	support
devise	construct	evaluate	attribute	obtain
assume	argue	reiterate	discover	decide

Using Verbs To Describe Phenomena

Which do you prefer: the phrase "to cut or split something into two theoretically and essentially equal parts" or the simple verb "bisect"? Which is easier to write and to read: the phrase "unite into what is essentially one body" or the simple verb "coalesce"? Your readers will be highly pleased with you if you offer them lively, precise, direct, robust, vibrant, single-word verbs, especially as you explain scientific phenomena. Furthermore, your writing will be less wordy and more direct and accurate. It is easy to be tempted in the other direction. Trying to sound impressive, it is easy to write "The sodar is prone to the submission of one pulse every 12 seconds" instead of the much simpler and more accurate "The sodar transmits one pulse every 12 seconds." Always beware of overcomplicating your verbs, and remember that their function is to describe actively and efficiently.

Many verbs are used continually in one field but rarely in another, so it is essential that you become familiar with those verbs that are standard vocabulary in your field. The verb "induce," which means "to produce an electric current or magnetic effect by induction," should be standard vocabulary for someone in physics or electrical engineering, while the verb "sinter," which means "to weld without melting," should be familiar and useful to those in metallurgy (it also doubles as a noun in geology).

Plenty of meaningful single-word verbs are out there just waiting for you to use them. One easy way to choose the best verb is to consult the brief (and certainly not exhaustive) list that follows to search for the kinds of active verbs that the best writers choose. The verbs are organized randomly to stress that they are not interchangeable nor arbitrary. Even though the exact verb that you need to describe a phenomenon may not be on this list, the verbs on the list do suggest the *kind* of verbs that you should choose. Many students keep this page open as they write a paper just to keep their minds tuned-in to using single-word active verbs. For efficiency, accuracy, and your own credibility as a scientist or engineer, always aim for the *best and simplest* verb. If you are unsure of a verb's exact meaning, be sure to look it up.

Active Verbs That Describe Phenomena

discharge	overlie	emanate	radiate	scatter
exchange	separate	surround	combine	eliminate
emit	transmit	carry	bombard	exert
exude	interact	behave	exchange	absorb
converge	extend	constrain	force	elongate
contract	trend	plunge	occur	fracture
continue	mix	slow	quicken	produce
bond	interlock	fuse	deteriorate	migrate
encompass	access	traverse	join	dominate
deposit	underlie	overlap	originate	isolate
invade	permeate	evolve	divide	sinter
reclaim	restore	abandon	contain	accrue
precede	influence	saturate	circulate	forecast
orient	distribute	allow	lag	terminate
activate	cease	record	form	transect
condense	enrich	invert	convert	alter
link	superimpose	rotate	rupture	streamline
appear	require	ascend	descend	collapse
superpose	crystallize	bisect	cede	coalesce
disperse	disseminate	disintegrate	propel	repel

Teachers actually get fired up about this issue. You may have had a frustrated (and frustrating?) professor write on your paper "Always use passive voice!" or "Never use passive voice!" during your studies, and your English textbook probably tells you that the active sentence "Jack hit the baseball" is better than the passive sentence "The baseball was hit by Jack." These bits of advice do not help much though, do they? You are not likely to have anyone named Jack hitting any baseballs in your papers, and obviously both passive and active voice are powerful tools in the right hands.

You are probably already able to identify whether or not sentences are written in the passive or active voice, but if not, here is a refresher: In the simplest terms, an active voice sentence is written in the form of "A does B." A passive voice sentence is written in the form of "A is done by B." Both are fine. In fact, notice how the sentences below, depending on the context in which they appear, are equally acceptable:

Passive voice —The rate of evaporation is controlled by the size of an opening.

Active voice —The size of an opening controls the rate of evaporation.

The passive choice slightly emphasizes "the rate of evaporation," while the active choice emphasizes "the size of an opening." Simple. So why all the fuss? Because the habit of overusing passive constructions rules too many writers, who automatically produce tangled sentences such as this one:

The Passive/ Active Voice Dilemma

> Groundwater flow is influenced by zones of fracture concentration, as can be recognized by the two model simulations (see Figures 1 and 2), by which one can see…

Forget it. The sentence is becoming a burden for the reader, and probably for the writer too. As often happens, the passive voice here has smothered potential verbs and kicked off a runaway train of prepositions. But the readers task gets much easier in the revised version below:

> Two model simulations (Figures 1 and 2) illustrate how zones of fracture concentration influence groundwater flow. These simulations show…

To revise the above, all I did was look for the two buried things (simulations and zones) in the original version that could actually do something, and I made the sentence clearly about these two nouns by placing them in front of active verbs. This is the general principle to follow as you compose in the active voice: put concrete nouns that can do something in front of active verbs.

But suppose you are writing a report where you may not use "I", or you are writing about a sentence subject that can not actually *do* anything. What to do when the passive voice is the best, most natural choice?

The answer lies in writing direct sentences—in passive voice—that have simple subjects and verbs. Compare the two sentences below:

> Photomicrographs were taken to allow easy comparison of the samples.

> Easy comparison of the samples was allowed by the taking of photomicrographs.

Both sentences are written in the passive voice, but for most ears the first sentence is more direct and understandable, and therefore preferable. Depending on the context, it does a better job of telling us what was done and why it was done. Especially if this sentence appears in the Experimental section of a report (and thus readers already know that the authors of the report took the photomicrographs), the first sentence neatly represents what the authors actually did—took photomicrographs—and why they did it—to allow easy comparison.

Passive voice is not really meant to create ambiguity or complicate wording. When you use the passive voice, seek economy and clarity. Avoid such empty and ambiguous phrases as "it might be thought that" (try "perhaps") or "it is to be supposed that" (try "presumably") or "the theory that is held by the writer of this report at the present time of this writing" (try "It is theorized that") or "one should think of" (try dropping it completely). You may worry that you are allowed to write only in the passive voice, but the passive can often be switched to the active without any rules being broken, and *both* the active and the passive voice can be direct, efficient, and clear. In your writing, you must strive to use both of them well.

When To Use The Active Voice

At least during your undergraduate studies, the nature of your writing assignments generally favors the active voice, because you usually write about general interest topics to educated laypeople and other scientists or engineers in a reader-friendly fashion. In general, a sentence that opens with a concrete simple subject followed by an active verb will serve you well; the rest of the sentence can reveal the new (and often necessarily wordy) information. What follows are two specific circumstances where passive voice is too often used, even though active voice is completely practical:

- Generally, use active voice in the topic sentences and the opening sentences of paragraphs—that way the topic for the paragraph is clearly announced:

    Crustal rocks contain an interesting historical record.

- When referring to another author's work or introducing a figure or table, it is often stylish and interpretive to put the author's name or the figure or table right into the subject of the sentence, then follow it with an active and literally correct verb:

    Feldman explains how the relative brightness of objects depends on the viewer's angle of observation.

    Figure 2 illustrates how fractal geometry can be used to create realistic landscapes.

What follows is an excerpt from a meteorology paper that proves how admirable and efficient the active voice can be. This paragraph is especially impressive in that it explains the complex concept of vorticity through an analysis of the seemingly ordinary phenomenon of smoke rings. Note the consistent use of simple precise subjects followed by active descriptive verbs:

Figure 4 depicts a smoke ring in which the layers of a toroidal vortex ring are visible. It is clear from the picture that the smoke ring moves away from its source and trails smoke from its center. The trail of smoke behind the moving smoke ring indicates that the same viscous stress that caused the smoke ring to form also causes its eventual destruction. As the smoke ring continues to move (Figure 5), the outside boundary of the ring rotates toward the same direction as the relative motion of the surrounding air. The inside boundary rotates opposite in direction, and thus the change in relative velocity with distance across the boundary produces drag.

Clearly, this is a paragraph that the writer toiled over, yet, thanks to the clear transitions and sensible use of the active voice, it is highly readable and efficient.

One cautionary note, though: even though you are generally allowed to use "I" or "we" in papers written largely in the active voice, you must beware of the temptation to overuse it. The word "apparently" can do the same job as "I believe that"; the word "however" is much better than "as I turn to another way of thinking about it." Also, using "I" can be distracting, especially because it might cause you to inject too much personal opinion or irrelevant persona—papers are not the place to share your irrelevant speculations or reveal your idiosyncrasies. Remember that your focus is on information and your considered interpretation of that information. Strong interpretive verbs or confident and accurate pronouncements automatically suggest that an "I" is at work anyway, so concentrate on choosing simple transitions, concrete nouns, and muscular verbs.

When To Use The Passive Voice

The passive voice is more commonly used on the graduate level than the undergraduate, but in some technical fields that involve a lot of lab work you may be using the passive voice regularly on the undergraduate level, particularly when you prepare technical reports based on labs you have completed. You might even be told never to use "I" or "we" in your papers. The convention of writing scientific reports largely in the passive voice is strong and sensible, and you should not fight it, but know how to work within the boundaries and not let it muddy up your thought process. When used correctly, the passive voice has the desired impact of focusing the reader's and writer's attention on the materials and the data, and it helps to foster objectivity, universality, and efficiency. This convention also helps writers to avoid using "we" over and over, so that strings of "we did this," "then we did this" do not appear.

Passive voice, couched within direct sentences containing simple subjects and verbs, is generally preferred in the following situations:

- Throughout the "Experimental" section of a scientific report, or anywhere that you must summarize your own or another author's experimental procedure or findings, but the actual inclusion of names would be awkward or distracting:

  Initially, a fractured steel specimen was plated with electroless nickel and secured in an epoxy mount by vacuum impregnation.

  The findings of the November 1991 report to NASA were based on DMTA, DSC, and FTIR test results.

- In formal abstracts (condensed summaries) that introduce papers:

Sensitivity experiments are reviewed to investigate the influence of Pacific sea surface temperature anomalies on blocking in the Northern Hemisphere.

- When it makes the most sense to emphasize the receiver of the action rather than the doer:

  The samples should be monitored regularly and should be dried carefully once they are cool.

  Winter wheat is planted in the autumn and ripens in the following spring or summer.

- When emphasis or variety demands it, or when the flow of your paragraph suggests that a passive construction is the most clear choice:

  One facet of multiple phase transformation can be seen through an examination of the gas gathering process. This process…

This section is devoted to those words that are commonly misused or overused in science and engineering. Certainly the words discussed here can and must be used at times, but you should make it your goal to use them frugally and carefully.

Will, Would, Can, Could

These four words deserve special attention because they are easily misused and overused. It is easy to forget that "would," "could," and "can" are almost always used hypothetically, and overusing them creates confusion. The problem is illustrated by these unintentionally misleading sentences from a draft for a mining engineering paper:

The roof of the mine would be characterized as being mostly clay and the floor would be characterized as being mostly claystone. Close inspection of the drill cores could be warranted to determine if there could be a gray shale bed above the coal seam.

After reading this, the frustrated reader is left with the questions "Are the roof and floor mostly clay or not?" and "Should we inspect the drill cores or not?". Rather than sounding accurate and firmly decisive, the writer comes off as hypothetical and wishy-washy, because the roof and floor are, after all, mostly clay. Note the wordiness that the repetition of "would be" creates as well. Here is the writer's revised version:

Both the roof and floor of the mine are mostly claystone. Close inspection of the drill cores is recommended to determine if there is a gray shale bed above the coal seam.

Much better: more decisive, direct, and shorter. The basic principle is this: only be hypothetical-sounding if you really are being hypo-

Commonly Overused Words

thetical. Challenge every "would," "could," and "can" that you use—see if you really mean "is" or "will." Also, remember that "can" is generally used to suggest a hypothetical present or potential, while "will" is usually used to suggest strong probability or future occurrence. This fact tells you to revise a sentence like the following one: "A comparison of MWD logs and wire line logs can be difficult because they will operate in different environments." In a revised version of this sentence, the writer should make it clear that the comparison of the two logs is difficult because the logs do operate in different environments.

Below are a few sentences in which "will," "would," "can," and "could" are correctly used:

Eventually these sediments will be deposited on a sea floor.
("Will" expresses strong probability and future likelihood.)

At still higher temperatures, the radiation would probably become stronger.

("Would" suggests hypothetical probability.)

Experiments have shown that polluted water can be purified by slow percolation through rocks and sediments.
("Can" suggests possibility and potential.)

These results suggest that low-energy photons could be causing the problem.
("Could" suggests possibility.)

In short, use "can," "could," and "would" to express possibility and hypothetical probability; use "will" to indicate strong probability and simple futurity. Beware especially of overusing "would"—once you jump on that train, it is difficult to get off.

Aspects

Do you find "aspects" a handy, satisfying word? Your reader does not. It is really an ineffectual word that suggests to your reader that you were too lazy to be more specific. Literally, an "aspect" is *the idea of a thought viewed by the mind,* in other words, *a thing.* Not so impressive after all then. Yet the word "aspect" seems to sound specific, especially in an introduction or in the opening sentences of a paragraph, inspiring thousands of people to write vacant sentences like "This paper will deal with many aspects of my topic," or "The problem has many aspects, and the first aspect is the most important aspect." These kinds of sentences just are not worth the ink. If the word "thing" is unacceptable (and it usually is) then "aspect" should be too. When you use "aspect" you usually mean a much more specific word such as *principle, property, factor, dilemma, development, reason, part.* To improve your style, you must write with literal meaning in mind—use the exact, most direct words that best convey your meaning.

To demonstrate the power of writing with literal meaning, here is some topnotch writing from the introductory paragraph of a geography paper:

> Interstate highway exits may all look the same on the high plains of western Kansas, but they are certainly not identical throughout the entire country. There are, however, elements of highway exits that are consistent and which do appear in similar form all over the country. I am not referring to the physical structure of the ramp systems and bridges of highway exits; their appearance is more a reflection of local topographic features and rights of way than of a specific design formula. The elements I am referring to are the commercial enterprises, businesses, and services that can be found at highway exits.

This writer had several opportunities to use the word "aspect," but he chose much more specific terms such as "structure," "reflection," "features," and "elements." Notice how he even took pains in the middle of the paragraph to analyze the specific elements that would *not* be a part of his paper, then he ended strongly on his theme: the specific elements of highway exits that he would analyze in his paper. Not a word was wasted.

In addition to avoiding the pitfalls of "aspect," you want to avoid other nonliteral and wordy phrases such as "the biggest reason for this" (just how BIG are reasons?), "at this particular point in time" (when else?), and "it is certainly very interesting to note that" (just prove it is interesting instead). In a word, use your words *literally*.

"This" And "It"

Do you want to annoy and confuse your readers? Then paste a paragraph together with "this" or "it" as a connecting word in nearly every sentence. Moreover, do not refer to anything specific with the "this" or "it"—keep the meaning vague. Without realizing it, many writers habitually plant a "this" or "it" wherever they sense that flow is needed. Most of the time when you use "this" or "it" you are actually referring to a specific noun or verb that is nearby, so it is vital that the reader knows which noun or verb you mean. One trick is to name whatever the "this" refers to immediately after it (i.e., "this phenomenon," "this principle," "this variation"). Note how much clearer the following sentences are because "this assumption" is used rather than just "this" by itself:

> The burial by thrusting is thought to occur rapidly. This assumption, however, is difficult to test.

Commonly, "it is" is overused as a sentence beginning. "It is this water that could become…" is better written as "This water could become… ." When the use of "it" is vague or unnecessary, try to simply eliminate the word.

The same principle holds true for words like "that" and "these": Do not overuse them, and when you do use them to refer to words in other sentences, be sure that the reader can easily tell exactly what other words you are referring to.

Feelings

Of course scientists and engineers have feelings, but use of the word "feelings" in your writing can lead to trouble. On a practical level, you do not have much room to use "feel" as a verb in your writing either. Phrases such as "I feel that the best answer is 3.2" or "we feel that this conclusion is correct" can draw large frowns from your readers. "Feel" has emotional connotations, and feelings are not a relevant part of rational conclusions in your writing (at least not on the page). Also, in a phrase such as "the drillstring feels the weight," the seemingly literal claim that an inanimate object such as a drillstring "feels" anything is clearly inaccurate. So handle the words "feel" and "feelings" with great care, and beware of writing in an overly subjective tone where you do not want one.

Special Stylistic Conventions Of Science and Engineering

There are a few special stylistic conventions worth attention here, especially since professors can be particularly sensitive to them. See the lessons in this section as opportunities to understand some of the standard rules of professional communication rather than as restrictions on your style. In technical writing, as in chess, it is safest to wield your creativity only within the rules.

Avoiding Sexist Language

From a stylistic standpoint, perhaps the best thing about the growing need for writers to guard against sexist language is that it forces them to explore the options that have always been available. By now everyone should be used to using Ms. rather than Miss or Mrs. in business letters and verbal communication, but it is time to go far beyond that. It is vital that you avoid sexist language when you write and give oral presentations, but if it just causes you to use "his/her" repeatedly then you are not living up to your obligations to keep your writing highly readable and efficient. Also, writing a sentence such as "Someone should lend their voice to this problem" is still grammatically unacceptable because "someone" is singular and "their" is plural. Most good writers attack the problem of sexist language in the following ways:

- By simply being more specific or creative (writing "humans" rather than "man").

- By using plural nouns rather than singular ones when appropriate ("scientists" rather than "a scientist"), or by avoiding gender-specific pronouns ("the author" rather than "he").

- By using forms of "he or she" (not "he/she") when it is not awkward or overly repetitive to do so.

- By changing some words to other parts of speech, thereby avoiding sexist pronouns ("walking" might work better than "he walked" as long as the grammar of the revision is sound).

With this in mind, consider the following example:

The consumer himself has the power to reduce fuel costs: If he sets his residential thermostat 2 degrees higher in the summer and 2 degrees lower in the winter, he saves energy.

In a revised version of this sentence, the sexist language of the original is avoided:

Consumers have the power to reduce fuel costs: By setting their residential thermostats 2 degrees higher in the summer and 2 degrees lower in the winter, they save energy.

Standard English usage still calls for the masculine form ("he" or "his") to refer correctly to either sex in writing, but rely on this only when you have to. Do not let your concern for sexist language cause your usage to be too unconventional ("personhole cover"? "personkind"?); instead, do exercise your options as a writer wisely, and remember that our language does change. Keep your eye on it.

Beware of Dangling Modifiers

Especially when you use passive voice, it is easy to create dangling modifiers—that is, descriptive words that seem to dangle off by themselves because they do not accurately describe the words next to them. Grammatically, if a sentence opens with a descriptive phrase before the subject, the phrase usually must directly explain the subject of the sentence or it becomes a dangling modifier. The following sentences contain dangling modifiers:

Using a viscometer, the pH was tested.

In determining the initial estimates, results from previous tests were used.

Grammatically, these two sentences are unacceptable, because the first implies that the *pH* used a viscometer, while the second implies that the *results themselves* came up with the initial estimates. The words that describe a sentence subject must be sensibly related to the subject, and in these two sentences that is not the case.

Revisions of the sentences to avoid dangling modifiers involve shuffling sentence parts around so that the meaning is more logical:

The pH was tested with a viscometer.

Results from previous tests were used to determine the initial estimates.

Particularly when you are writing a technical report, or anytime when you must use the passive voice regularly, take special care to watch out for dangling modifiers.

Unsplitting Infinitives

A split infinitive is a phrase in which one or more words are placed between the word "to" and its accompanying verb. "To carefully place" is a split infinitive because "carefully" is interrupting the more basic phrase "to place." Many writers choose to split infinitives, but in science and engineering it is frowned upon, and if you do it habitually you could end up putting the "to" and the verb too far away from each other, thus causing confusion. The following sentence contains a split infinitive:

The plastic contains a catalyst that causes it to completely and naturally disappear in a few months.

In the more acceptable version of the sentence, the "to" and the verb are brought together:

The plastic contains a catalyst that causes it to disappear completely and naturally in a few months.

Usually, the words that split an infinitive can go outside the infinitive or be omitted altogether. Keep your eyes peeled for split infinitives; many of your professors will.

Contractions Not Welcome

Contractions—in which an apostrophe is used to "contract" two words into one by joining parts of them—are considered to be informal, conversational expression. In the formal writing that you will be doing for your classes, or as you submit formal work for an editor's or superior's perusal, you simply do not have the option of using contractions unless you are quoting something that contains contractions. Some bosses even hate them in inter-office memos. If you use contractions you will come off as sloppy and unprofessional. The safest idea is to avoid them entirely. If you avoid them, you will discover that your writing becomes more emphatic and favors the active voice, so the benefits are direct. Especially watch out for the contractions "it's," "we've," "you're," and "who's." Apostrophes that show possession (i.e., the apostrophe in "a pixel's value") are, of course, used frequently, but remember that apostrophes that contract two words signal that the two words can and should be written out separately.

Textual References To Temperature Measurements

Degree measures of temperature are normally expressed with the ° symbol rather than by the written word:

The sample was heated to 80° C.

Unlike the abbreviations for Fahrenheit and Celsius, the abbreviation for Kelvin (which refers to an absolute scale of temperature) is not preceded by the degree symbol (i.e., 12 K is correct).

Textual References To Numbers

The rules for expressing numbers in science and engineering are simple and straightforward:

- All important measured quantities—particularly those involving decimal points, dimensions, degrees, distances, weights, measures, and sums of money—should be expressed in numeral form (e.g., 1.3 seconds, $25,000, 2 amperes).

- Counted numbers of ten or less should be written out.

- If possible, a sentence should not begin with a number, but if it does the number should be written out.

- Treat similar numbers in grammatically connected groups alike.

Following these rules, here are some examples of properly expressed numbers:

The depth to the water at the time of testing was 16.16 feet.

For this treatment, the steel was heated 18 different times.

Two dramatic changes followed: four samples exploded and thirteen lab technicians resigned.

Punctuation, Capitalization, and Spelling

> *If you take hyphens seriously you will surely go mad.*
> —*Anonymous*

It is amazing how consistently we repeat the exact same little errors, but we truly can correct them by identifying them as patterns and writing with an eye for our particular habits. As a graduate student, I misspelled the word "separate" 16 times on an exam and the professor kindly circled the offending letter each time, even counting the number of times I had misspelled it and noting this glibly in an end comment by saying "I wish you could spell better." His chiding cured me and I have not misspelled "separate" since. Many students find that they have picked up the habit of putting commas in automatically before prepositions or even *after* conjunctions rather than before, which can actually mislead the reader, halting the proper flow of a sentence. Once such habits are identified, however, they can be addressed effectively.

Those annoying little details about punctuation, capitalization, and spelling are important to master, and even with the spell checker eternally activated, our errors do make it onto the page and affect our reader's assessment of our work. I know of an engineer whose lazy proofreading has sometimes caused him to report inaccurate dollar amounts to a client. A scientist who mistakenly capitalizes all of the letters in "Btu" does not appear to realize that it stands for "British thermal unit." And capitalization rules can be highly important to meaning: a student in geosciences, for example, must be aware of whether or not to capitalize "ice age" (*yes* when you mean the specific glacial epoch; no when you mean a general reference to any of a series of cold periods alternating with periods of relative warmth).

So work on the little things. Seek to understand punctuation as a grammatical unit, and accept proper spelling and capitalization as professional necessities. This chapter will help you to do so without immersing you into a grammatical swamp.

Chapter 3

Quotation Marks

Despite what you may see practiced—especially in advertising, on television, and even in business letters—the fact is that the period and comma go *inside* the quotation marks almost all of the time. Confusion arises because the British system is different, and the American system may automatically look wrong to you, but it is simply one of the frequently broken rules of written English in America: the period and comma go inside the quotation marks.

Hence: The people of the pine barrens are often called "pineys."

Not: The people of the pine barrens are often called "pineys".

However, the semicolon, colon, dash, question mark, and exclamation point fall *outside* of the quotation marks (unless, of course, the quoted material has internal punctuation of its own).

This measurement is commonly known as "dip angle"; dip angle is the angle formed between a normal plane and a vertical.

Built only 30 years ago, Shakhtinsk – "minetown" – is already seedy.

When she was asked the question "Are rainbows possible in winter?" she answered by examining whether raindrops freeze at temperatures below 0° C. (Quoted material has its own punctuation.)

Hyphens

It is vital that you use hyphens properly; they help you to write efficiently and concretely and you will have to use them regularly because of the nature of technical writing. The hyphen is a JOINER. It joins:

- two nouns to make one complete word (kilogram-meter);

- an adjective and a noun to make a compound word (accident-prone);

- two words that, when linked, describe a noun (well-developed plan, two-dimensional object);

- a prefix with a noun (un-American);

- double numbers (twenty-four);

- "self" words (self-employed, self-conscious);

- ethnic labels (Irish-American);

- new word blends (cancer-causing, cost-effective).

The only easy rule to apply when using the hyphen is that the resulting word must act as *one unit;* therefore, the hyphen creates a new word—either a noun or a modifier—that has a single meaning. Usually, you can tell whether you need a hyphen by applying common sense and mentally excluding one of the words, testing how the words would work together without the hyphen. For example, the phrases "high-pressure system," "water-repellent surface," and "fuel-efficient car" would not make sense without hyphens, because you would not refer to a "high system," a "water surface," or a "fuel car."

Here are some examples of properly used hyphens:

small-scale study
two-prong plug
strength-to-weight ratio
high-velocity flow
well-known example
vice-president
self-employed worker
one-third majority
coarse-grained wood
decision-making process
blue-green algae
silver-stained cells
protein-calorie malnutrition
membrane-bound vesicles
phase-contrast microscope

It is important to use punctuation marks both properly and to your advantage. Remember that punctuation marks are silent allies, and you can exploit them as such. Punctuation marks do not just indicate sound patterns—they are symbols that clarify grammatical structure and sentence meaning. What follows are some basics about some of the most powerful and most commonly used punctuation marks.

Semicolons, Colons, and Dashes

The Semicolon

The semicolon is commonly misused in scientific writing; in fact, it is often confused with the colon. Grammatically, the semicolon almost always functions as AN EQUAL SIGN; it says that the two parts being joined are relatively equal in their length and have the same grammatical structure. Also, the semicolon helps you to LINK TWO THINGS WHOSE INTERDEPENDENCY YOU WANT TO ESTABLISH. The sentence parts on either side of the semicolon tend to depend on each other for complete meaning. Use the semicolon when you wish to create or emphasize a generally equal or even interdependent relationship between two things. Note the interdependent relationship of the two sentence parts linked by the semicolon in this example:

The sonde presently used is located in the center of the borehole; this location enables the engineer to reduce microphonics and standoff sensitivity.

The semicolon is also handy for SEPARATING A SERIES OF PARALLEL ITEMS that could otherwise be confused with each other.

As an engineering assistant, I had a variety of duties: participating in pressure ventilation surveys; drafting, surveying, and data compilation; acting as a company representative during a roof-bolt pull test.

The Colon

The colon is like a road sign; it ANNOUNCES THAT SOME-THING IMPORTANT IS COMING. It acts as an arrow pointing forward, telling you to read on for important information. Use the colon to introduce material that explains, amplifies, or summaries what has preceded it.

In low carbon steels, banding tends to affect two properties in particular: tensile ductility and yield strength.

The colon is also commonly used to present a list, which comes in handy when there is a lot of similar material to join:

A compost facility may not be located as follows: within 300 feet of an exceptional-value wetland; within 100 feet of a perennial stream; within 50 feet of a property line.

The Dash

The dash—which is typed as a hyphen with a blank space on both sides, or as one long bar if your keyboard offers it—functions almost as a colon does in that it adds to the preceding material, but it is actually a bit more sophisticated. Like a caesura (a timely pause) in music, a dash INDICATES A STRONG PAUSE, THEN GIVES EXTRA EMPHASIS TO WHATEVER FOLLOWS THAT PAUSE. In effect, a dash allows you to REDEFINE what was just written, making it more explicit. You can also use a dash as it is used in the first sentence of this paragraph: to frame a parenthetical-type comment that you do not want to de-emphasize.

Jill Emery confirms that Muslim populations have typically been ruled by non-Muslims—specifically Americans, Russians, Israelis, and the French.

The dissolution took 20 minutes—longer than anticipated—but measurements were begun as soon as the process was completed.

Commas

These little demons increase and trivialize the nightmares of many a professor after an evening of reading student papers. A sure way to irritate educated readers of your work is to give them an overabundance of opportunities to address your comma problems. It is easy but dangerous to take the attitude that Sally once did in a *Peanuts* comic strip, asking Charlie Brown to correct her essay by showing her "where to sprinkle in the little curvy marks."

You have probably heard the common tips on using commas: "Use one wherever you would naturally use a pause" or "Read your work aloud, and whenever you feel yourself pausing, put in a comma." These techniques help to a degree, but our ears tend to trick us and we need other avenues of attack. Also, it seems impossible to remember or apply the 17 or so grammatical explanations of comma usage that you were probably forced to learn way back in 8th grade. (For example: "Use commas to set off independent clauses joined by the common coordinating conjunctions... Put a comma before the coordinating conjunction in a series.") Perhaps the best and most instructive way, then, for us to approach the comma is to remember its fundamental function: it is a SEPARATOR. Knowing this, it is useful to determine what sorts of things generally require separation. In sum, commas are used to separate COMPLETE IDEAS, DESCRIPTIVE PHRASES, ADJACENT ITEMS, and before and after most TRANSITION WORDS.

Comma Rules

COMPLETE IDEAS need to be separated by a comma because, by definition, they could be grammatically autonomous, but the writer is choosing to link them. Complete ideas are potentially whole sentences that the writer chooses to link with a conjunction such as "and" or "but."

Digital recordings made it possible to measure the nuclear magnetic signal at any depth, and this allowed for a precise reading to be taken at every six inches.

DESCRIPTIVE PHRASES often need to be separated from the things that they describe in order to clarify that the descriptive phrases are subordinate. Descriptive phrases tend to come at the very beginning of a sentence, right after the subject of a sentence, or at the very end of a sentence.

Near the end of the eighteenth century, James Hutton introduced a point of view that radically changed scientists' thinking about geologic processes.

James Lovelock, who first measured CFCs globally, said in 1973 that CFCs constituted no conceivable hazard.

All of the major industrialized nations approved, making the possibility a reality.

ADJACENT ITEMS are words or phrases that have some sort of parallel relationship. They are separated so that the reader can see each item individually. In the second example that follows, the dates July 4 and 1968 are parallel. In the third example, the three phrases, all beginning with different verbs, are parallel.

Weathering may extend only a few centimeters beyond the zone in fresh granite, metamorphic rocks, sandstone, shale, and other rocks.

The river caught fire on July 4, 1968, in Cleveland, Ohio.

This approach increases homogeneity, reduces the heating time, and creates a more uniform microstructure.

Finally, TRANSITION WORDS add new viewpoints to your material; commas before and after most transition words help to separate ideas as well as establish the relationship between them. Transition words tend to appear at the beginning or in the middle of a sentence. Typical transition words that require commas before and after them include *however, thus, therefore, also,* and *nevertheless.*

Therefore, the natural gas industry can only be understood fully through an analysis of these recent political changes.

The lead precursor was prepared, however, by reacting pure lead acetate with sodium isopropoxide.

The Comma Before an "And" Dilemma

It is true that commas are sometimes optional, and the question of when to put a comma before an "and" can be puzzling. If you have a lengthy sentence that includes two distinct subjects and verbs connected by an "and"—as in the first sentence of this paragraph—then certainly you must put a comma before the "and." However, you need not necessarily put a comma before the "and" in a list of three items or more. Therefore, writing "I am industrious, resourceful and loyal" is correct. But be careful: If the list of three or more things is made up of phrases (small groups of words), you must place a comma before the "and" that introduces the last phrase to avoid confusing the reader.

The latest logging tools include an array induction imager, an array seismic imager, and a combinable seismic imager.

Killing the Comma

Perhaps the best way to troubleshoot your particular comma problems, especially if they are serious, is to identify and understand the patterns of your errors. We tend to make the same mistakes over and over again; in fact, many writers develop the unfortunate habit of automatically putting commas into places such as these:

- between the subject and verb of a sentence
- after any number
- before any preposition
- before or after any conjunction

Thus, incorrect sentences such as these appear in papers:

The bushings, must be adjusted weekly, to ensure that the motor is not damaged.

Many geologists still do not fully appreciate these findings even after 22 years, following the publication of the discovery paper.

Other manufactured chemicals that also contain bromine are superior for extinguishing fires in situations where people, and electronics are likely to be present.

The price of platinum will rise, or fall depending on several distinct factors.

If any of the above commas looks fine to you then you may be in the habit of using commas incorrectly, and you will need to attack your specific habits, perhaps even in a routine, repetitive fashion, in order to break yourself of them. Similarly, it is common for someone to have to look up the same tricky word dozens of times before committing its proper spelling to memory. As with spelling, commas (or the absence of commas) must be repeatedly challenged in your writing. As you perfect your comma usage you are also recognizing and reevaluating your sentence patterns, and the rewards are numerous. There is no foolproof or easy way to exorcise all of your comma demons, but following the preceding guidelines is a good start. In the end, you simply have got to make a habit of reading, writing, and revising with comma correctness in mind.

Capitalization

As a student in the sciences or engineering, who must often refer to such things as geographic locations, company names, temperature scales, and processes or apparatuses named after people, it is vital that you capitalize consistently and accurately. What follows are ten fundamental rules for capitalization. Check out the first rule. It gets fumbled in papers all the time.

- Capitalize the names of major portions of your paper and all references to major items created in your paper (such as figures, tables, or airshafts). NOTE: Some journals do not follow this rule, but most do.

my Introduction	Airshaft 3
see Figure 4	Table 1
Appendix A	Graph 6

- Capitalize the names of definite regions, localities, and political divisions.

Wheeling Township	the French Republic
Lancaster County	the United Kingdom
the Wheat Belt	the Arctic Circle

- Capitalize the names of highways, routes, bridges, buildings, monuments, parks, ships, automobiles, hotels, forts, dams, railroads, and major coal and mineral deposits.

Highway 13	Route 1
Michigan Avenue	the White House
Alton Railroad	the Statue of Liberty
Herrin No. 6 seam	the Queen Elizabeth

- Capitalize the proper names of persons, places and their derivatives, and geographic names (continents, countries, states, cities, oceans, rivers, mountains, lakes, harbors, and valleys).

Howard Pickering	Great Britain
Chicago	British
New York Harbor	Gulf of Mexico
Rocky Mountains	Pennsylvania
Aleutian Islands	the Aleutian low

- Capitalize the names of historic events and documents, government units, political parties, business and fraternal organizations, clubs and societies, companies, and institutions.

the Second Amendment	the Civil War
Congress	Bureau of Mines
Republicans	Ministry of Energy

- Capitalize titles of rank when they are joined to a person's name, and the names of stars and planets. NOTE: The names earth, sun, and moon are not normally capitalized, although they may be capitalized when used in connection with other bodies of the solar system.

Professor Bise	President Thomas
Milky Way	Venus

- Capitalize words named after geographic locations, the names of major historical or geological time frames, and most words derived from proper names. NOTE: The only way to be sure if a word derived from a person's name should be capitalized is to look it up in the dictionary. "Bunsen burner" (after Robert Bunsen) is capitalized while "diesel engine" (after Rudolph Diesel) is not. ALSO: referring to specific geologic time frames, The Chicago Manual of Style says not to capitalize the words "era," "period," and "epoch," but the American Association of Petroleum Geologists says that these words should be capitalized. I choose to capitalize them, as those who write in the geological sciences should by convention.

Coriolis force	Fourier coefficients
English tweeds	Walker Circulation
Hadley cell	Petri dish
Boyle's law	Russell volumeter
Planck's constant	Klinkenberg effect
Middle Jurassic Period	Mesozoic Era
the Industrial Revolution	the Inquisition

- Capitalize references to temperature scales, whether written out or abbreviated.

10° F	Fahrenheit degrees
20° C	Celsius degrees

- Capitalize references to major sections of a country or the world.

the Near East	the South

- Capitalize the names of specific courses, the names of languages, and the names of semesters.

Anatomy 20	French
Spring semester	Fall term, 1992

- Do not capitalize the names of the seasons, unless the seasons are personified, as in poetry (Spring's breath).

spring	winter

- Do not capitalize the words north, south, east, and west when they refer to directions.

We traveled west.	The sun rises in the east.

- In general, do not capitalize words that have come to have specialized meaning, even though their origins are in words that are capitalized.

navy blue	india ink
pasteurization	biblical

- Do not capitalize the names of elements.

tungsten	nitrogen

- Do not capitalize words that are used so frequently and informally that they have come to have highly generalized meaning.

north pole	big bang theory
arctic climate	midwesterner

Common Capitalization Errors

Spell Checking

Word processing on computers gets easier and easier to do, and with the growing access to laser printers, things such as theses, figures, tables, resumes, and cover letters can be made to look especially spiffy. Using software also makes revision of your work much simpler, empowering you to move around blocks of text in a snap, and allowing you to use slightly different versions of cover letters and resumes with minimal retyping. With all the spell checkers and grammar checkers out there, you can make your spelling and grammar closer to perfect as well. All good news.

But all this nifty stuff has a price. Just as so many of us rely on calculators to do all our math for us—even to the point that we do not trust calculations done by our own hand—far too many of us use spell checkers as proofreaders, and we ultimately use them to justify laziness. I once received a complaint from an outraged professor that a student had continually misspelled "miscellaneous" as "mescaline" (the drug). The student's spell checker did not pick up the error, but the professor certainly did, and he told me that he even speculated privately that the student who wrote the paper did so while on mescaline.

So proceed with caution when using spell checkers and grammar checkers. They are not gods, and they do not substitute for meticulous proofreading and clear thinking. There is an instructive moment in a M*A*S*H episode, when Father Mulcahy complains to Colonel Potter about a typo in a new set of Bibles—one of the commandments reads "thou shalt commit adultery." Father sheepishly worries aloud that "These lads are taught to follow orders." For want of a single word the meaning is lost.

If used properly, grammar checkers make you work *harder* on your writing and force you to reconsider your sentence patterns, but they can also easily mislead you into making a grammatical error if you are not careful. In many ways, word processing magic does make things easier, but do not allow it to make you irresponsible, or to appear so.

Spelling Rules

I have a crusty little spelling dictionary (1) published in 1964 that I still use frequently. I adapted the six basic spelling rules that appear below from that dictionary. Even without memorizing the rules, you can improve your spelling simply by reviewing them and scanning the examples and exceptions until the fundamental concepts begin to sink in. When in doubt, always look up the word.

- In words ending with a silent e, you usually drop the e before a suffix that begins with a vowel.

survive + al	=	survival
divide + ing	=	dividing
fortune + ate	=	fortunate

Common Exceptions:

manageable	singeing	mileage
advantageous	dyeing	acreage
peaceable	canoeing	lineage

- In words ending with a silent *e*, you usually retain the *e* before a suffix than begins with a consonant.

```
arrange + ment    =    arrangement
forgive + ness    =    forgiveness
safe + ty         =    safety
```

Common Exceptions:

```
ninth (from nine)       argument  (from argue)
wisdom (from wise)      wholly  (from whole)
```

- In words of two or more syllables that are accented on the final syllable and end in a single consonant preceded by a single vowel, you double the final consonant before a suffix beginning with a vowel.

```
refer + ing       =    referring
regret + able     =    regrettable
```

However, if the accent is not on the last syllable, the final consonant is not doubled.

```
benefit + ed      =    benefited
audit + ed        =    audited
```

- In words of one syllable ending in a single consonant that is preceded by a single vowel, you double the final consonant before a suffix that begins with a vowel. (It sounds more complex than it is; just look at the examples.)

```
big + est         =    biggest
hot + er          =    hotter
bag + age         =    baggage
```

- In words ending in *y* preceded by a consonant, you usually change the *y* to *i* before any suffix that does not begin with an *i*.

```
beauty + ful      =    beautiful
accompany + ment  =    accompaniment
accompany + ing   =    accompanying (suffix begins
                         with i)
```

If the final *y* is preceded by a vowel, however, the rule does not apply.

```
journeys      obeying       essays
buys          repaying      attorneys
```

- Use *i* before *e* except when the two letters follow *c* and have an *e* sound, or when they have an a sound as in neighbor and weigh.

i before e (*e* sound)	**e before i (*a* sound)**
shield	vein
believe	weight
grieve	veil
mischievous	neighbor

weird	foreign	forfeit
either	ancient	neither
sovereign	siege	height
seize	surfeit	leisure

Commonly Misspelled Words

If you do find yourself overrelying on spell checkers or misspelling the same word for the 17th time this year, it would obviously be to your advantage to improve your spelling. One shortcut to doing this is to consult the following list of words that are frequently used and misspelled. Many writers even put a mark next to a word whenever they have to look it up, thereby helping themselves identify those fiendish words that give them the most trouble.

abandon	abandoned	abundant	absence
academic	academically	accelerator	accept
acceptable	accessible	accidentally	accommodate
accompanied	accompanying	accomplish	accumulate
accuracy	accustomed	achievement	acknowledge
acknowledgment	acquaintance	acquire	acquit
acre	acreage	across	actually
address	admission	admittance	adolescent
adolescence	advantageous	advertisement	aerial
against	aggravate	aggressive	aisle
a lot (never *alot*)	allotting	almost	already
always	amateur	among	amount
analysis	analyze	ancestry	announcement
annual	apparatus	apparent	apparently
appearance	appreciate	appropriate	appropriately
approximate	approximately	arctic	arguing
argument	article	artistically	association
athlete	athletic	attendance	attitude
awful	awkward		
balance	bankruptcy	bargain	basically
battalion	beautiful	becoming	before
beginning	believe	beneficial	benefited
biased	biggest	boundary	Britain
bulletin	bureaucratic	business	
calendar	camouflage	candidate	career
careful	category	ceiling	challenge
channel	chaos	character	characteristics
chief	chiefly	choose	chose
chosen	clothes	clothing	coarse
column	coming	commercial	commission
commitment	committee	communism	communists
compel	compelled	competition	completely
concede	conceivable	condemn	condemned
conferred	confused	connoisseur	conscience
conscientious	conscious	consists	continuous
controlled	controlling	controversial	convenient

coolly	criticism	crowded	cruelty
curiosity	curriculum		
dealt	deceive	decision	deferred
definite	definitely	definition	descend
description	desirable	desperate	develop
different	dilemma	disagree	disappear
disappoint	disapprove	disaster	disastrous
discern	discipline	discussion	dispel
disservice	dissipate	distinct	duly
during			
echoes	efficiency	efficient	eighth
eliminate	ellipse	embarrass	eminent
empty	endeavor	enemy	enthusiastically
entirely	entrance	environment	equipment
equipped	especially	essential	except
excellent	excess	existence	experience
explanation	extremely		
fallacy	familiar	family	fascinate
fascism	favorite	February	fiery
finally	financial	financially	fission
fluorine	foreign	foresee	foreseeable
forfeit	forty	forward	fourth
frantically	friend	fulfill	
generally	genius	government	grammar
grammatically	grandeur	Great Britain	grievance
guarantee	guerrilla	guidance	
handicapped	happily	harass	heard
height	here	hindrance	hoping
hopeless	humorous	hundred	hurriedly
hygiene	hypocrisy	hypocrite	
ideally	ignorant	illogical	imagine
imitate	immediately	immense	impossible
incidentally	independent	individually	ingenious
initially	initiative	innocent	innocuous
inoculate	intellectual	intelligence	intelligent
insistent	interest	interfered	interference
interrupt	iridescent	irrelevant	irreplaceable
jewelry	judgment	judicial	
knowledge	knowledgeable		
laboratory	later	lenient	liable
liaison	library	lightning	likely
listening	literature	loneliness	loose
lose	lying		
magazine	maintenance	manageable	maneuver
manual	marriage	mathematics	meant
medicine	medieval	mileage	millennium

miniature	miscellaneous	mischievous	missile
misspelled	mortgage	muscle	
narrative	naturally	necessary	necessity
nineteen	ninety	ninth	noticeable
noticing	nuclear	nuisance	numerous
occasion	occasionally	occur	occurred
occurring	occurrence	official	omission
omit	omitted	oneself	operate
opinion	opponent	opportunity	opposite
oppression	ordinarily	originally	
pamphlet	paraffin	parallel	parliament
particular	particularly	pastime	peaceable
peculiar	perceive	permissible	perseverance
persistence	pollute	pollution	population
possess	possession	possible	possibly
practically	preference	preferred	prejudice
prejudiced	primitive	privilege	probably
proceed	procedure	profession	professor
publicly	purpose		
quantify	quantity	quiet	quite
realize	rebellion	recede	receive
recession	recommend	reference	referring
remembrance	reservoir	rhythm	ridiculous
saccharine	sacrifice	safety	satellite
schedule	scientists	scintillate	separate
sergeant	shepherd	shining	shrubbery
similar	sincerely	sophomore	souvenir
specifically	statistics	strenuous	stretch
stubbornness	subtle	subtly	succeed
success	succession	succinct	sufficient
summary	summation	summed	supersede
supposed	suppress	surely	surprise
surrounding	syllable	symmetry	symmetrical
tariff	technique	temperament	temperature
their	therefore	thorough	though
through	tobacco	tomorrow	tragedy
transferred	trespass	truly	Tuesday
twelfth	tyranny		
unanimous	unconscious	uncontrollable	undoubtedly
unforeseen	unmistakably	unnatural	unnecessary
until	usable	useful	usually
vacuum	valuable	various	vegetable
vehicle	vengeance	villain	violence
visible			
warring	weather	Wednesday	weird
where	whether	whistle	wholly
whose	writing	written	

abrasive	absorption	aggregate	Aleutian
algae	algorithm	alkali	alkyl
analogous	angular	anomalous	anomaly
aperture	aquatic	aqueous	aquifer
asbestos	asymmetry		
bandwidth	base line	blackbody	brackish
buoyancy	buoyant		
capacitance	Celsius	cetacean	chromatography
clear-cut	climatology	coaxial	combustible
condensation	conductivity	configuration	corollary
corrosion	crustacean	crustal	crystalline
crystallography			
data base	deposition	diffraction	diffusion
discrete	dissymmetry	divisible	Doppler effect
Doppler radar	drainage		
ebullient	ebullition	eigenfunction	eigenvalue
emission	emissivity	end point	equilibrium
equinox	evaporation	eyepiece	
facies change	Fahrenheit	feedback	ferromagnetism
ferrous	filterable	flow chart	fluorescence
fluorescent	Fourier series	Fresnel equations	
geyser	glacial	gradient	
half-life	halogen	hatchable	heat-treat
histogram	histology	horsepower	hybridization
hydraulic	hysteresis		
in situ	incandescent	infinitesimal	inflection
infrared	interference	isotropic	isotropism
least squares	logarithm	luminance	luminescence
luminescent	luminosity	luminous	
manganese	mean life	measurable	metallurgical
metallurgy	midpoint	monetary	
Newton's law	nucleation	nuclei	
opaque	operable	optical	orogeny
oscillation			
parameter	peninsula	permeability	Petri dish
phosphorus	photo-ionization	photocell	piezoelectric
Planck's constant	plateau	polarization	polygon
polymerization	porosity	precipitation	predominant
radiant	radio frequency	radioactive	radiocarbon
refractive	resistant	resistivity	retardance
reversible	rock salt		
salinity	seismic	side band	sinusoidal
solenoid	solid state	soluble	space-time

Commonly Misspelled Terminology

spectrometer	spectroscopy	steam-distilled	stochastic
strata	stratigraphic	stratigraphy	subsidence
terranes	test tube	tidal	tonnage
tornadoes	transit time	transmissible	transmissivity
transmittance	troposphere	trough	typhoon
un-ionized			
valence	viscometer	viscosimeter	viscosity
viscous	visible		
wave front	wave packet	wave system	wave theory
wavelength	wettability		
xenolith			

Commonly Misused Terms

Writing isn't hard; no harder than ditch-digging.
—Patrick Dennis

This chapter is for everyone. We have all made the mistakes that are described herein. How many times have you found yourself puzzling over the distinction between "affect" and "effect," "it's" and "its"? It is not surprising that we maintain such uncertainties, because in any town in America you can find billboards and road signs and ads and newspapers with outright usage errors printed boldly for all to see. Keep watch and you will spot errors such as these:

"Man Alright After Crocodile Attack" ("Alright" should be "All Right")

"Auction at This Sight: One Week" ("Sight" should be "Site")

"This Line Ten Items or Less" ("Less" should be "Fewer")

"Low Prices Everyday" ("Everyday" should be "Every Day")

Perhaps there is little need here to preach about the value of the material in this chapter. Quite simply, there is a correct way and an incorrect way to use words, and you should make it your business to learn the rules for the trickiest and most misused terms. You can also dig up style handbooks with lessons on especially tricky terminology within your discipline. For instance, *Writing in Earth Science,* by Robert Bates (1), gives advice on using such terms as "areal," "lithology," "terrane," and "zone." Never hesitate to look up a term for its proper usage if you can—there is a lot to be said for being correct.

Accept/Except

Accept is a verb meaning receive with consent:

Paraguay did not accept the proposed solution.

Except is sometimes a verb (meaning *exclude*) but it is more commonly used just as the word *but* is used:

We could verify all of the important factors except one.

Affect/Effect

Affect is a verb. Think of the "a" in "affect" standing for "active verb." To *affect* is to influence:

Chapter 4

The moon affects the tides.

Effect is usually a noun, and it means *outcome or result:*

Inflation is one of the effects of war.

Things can also have *effects* on other things:

Brackish water has negative effects on certain vegetation.

Finally—to the horror of many—effect can also be used as a verb to mean to bring about, as in the phrase "to effect a change."

Alot

Alot is never correct. It is supposed to be two words; therefore: *a lot.* Never write a note to your professor at the end of the semester saying that you really learned *alot.*

Alright

All wrong. *Alright* is listed in most dictionaries as a common misspelling of what should be two words. In your writing, use *all right.*

Alternate/Alternative

As an adjective, *alternate* means *every other,* and it is usually used in relation to time or objects:

We were asked to focus on alternate lines of the figure. (Every other one.)

Alternate is also a verb, meaning to *switch back and forth in turns:*

The wet season alternates with the dry season.

Alternative denotes that *a choice was made* between at least two things:

Alternative paths were chosen.

Among/Between

Among is appropriate when *more than two things* are involved:

Deforestation is among the world's environmental problems.

Between is used to describe a relationship involving *only two things:*

A satisfactory agreement was reached between the two countries.

Current usage also permits *between* when each entity is considered individually in relation to the others:

Between them, each client agreed that this solution was best.

Amount of/Number of

Amount of works with *noncountables; number of* works with *countables:*

The amount of heat is lowered every three minutes. ("Heat" is non-countable.)

A number of toggle switches were installed. ("Toggle switches" are countable.)

Area/Region/Section

Use *region* for *large geographic units* and *area* for *smaller ones.* Also, keep your usage consistent—the "region" of one paragraph should not become the "area" of another.

There is one compost facility located in the township area, but three located in nearby regions.

Section is best reserved for land sections and cross-sections.

Six sections were successfully mapped last year.

As/Like

These two words are not interchangeable. *As* means *to the same extent, degree,* or *in the way that:*

The engine responds as it should.

Like means *similar to:*

The spadix of a jack-in-the-pulpit looks like a club.

Assure/Ensure/Insure

Thankfully, these three verbs are nearly interchangeable. All three mean to *make secure or certain.* The distinction is that *assure* is generally used to refer to *someone having a belief reinforced:*

She assured me that I was correct.

Insure is favored in instances of *guaranteeing life or property against risk:*

I insured my new business.

But broader circumstances allow for much more flexibility. Results can *ensure* or *insure* success, for instance.

Between...and/From...to/—

These combinations are not interchangeable. Normally, *between* and *to* can not be joined, nor can *from* and *and.* Therefore, "between x and y" or "from x to y" is correct, but "between x to y" or "from x and y" is incorrect. Also, the *hyphen* between two values (such as "5-10") functions invisibly as the word *to*, but it should only be used alone. Therefore, "It moved 5-10 meters" is correct but "It moved from 5-10 meters" or "It moved between 5-10 meters" is not.

Cite/Site/Sight

Cite is a verb meaning *to mention* or *to make reference to:*

She cited the Journal of Atmospheric Sciences in her paper.

Site is a noun meaning *location:*

Raleigh is the site of the new mine.

Sight is both a noun and a verb that refers to *seeing:*

We sighted the white smoke plumes before we reached the lime mine. It was quite a sight.

Compare to/Compare with

To *compare to* is to suggest resemblances between things that have *essentially different natures:*

Ocean waves can be compared to cake frosting.

To *compare with* is to suggest resemblances between things that have *essentially similar natures:*

Saturn can be compared with Jupiter.

A solid rule that will help you to choose the proper phrase is that *compare with* applies when there are *two entities that can be measured by a common standard.* For example, it is correct to say that "particles are small compared with the wavelength of the light illuminating them," because "particles" and "wavelength" are measured by the same standard.

Compose/Constitute/Include

To *compose* or *constitute* is *to form* or *to make up:*

Three parts constitute the whole.

The formation is composed of limestone and shale.

Include indicates a selective, incomplete listing of constituents, implying that there are other constituents as well:

The formation includes limestone and shale. (Other constituents are implied.)

Comprise

Literally, to *comprise* is to *include* or *contain*. The earth comprises rocks (it includes them), but rocks do not comprise the earth (they do not include it). Therefore:

The Union comprises 50 states.

The whole comprises the parts, but not vice versa.

Strict writers say that using *comprise* in the passive ("The Union is comprised of 50 states") is unacceptable.

Continual/Continuous

Continual denotes *intermittent activity; continuous* means *unceasing, uninterrupted activity.* Meals are *continual;* time is *continuous.*

Different than/Different from

Established usage says that *different than* is not correct; *different from* is:

Oxygen is different from nitrogen.

e.g./et al./i.e.

It is important to use these abbreviations literally and to punctuate them correctly. Many writers confuse *e.g.* and *i.e.,* and many type *et al.* improperly or do not realize what it actually stands for.

The abbreviation *e.g.* is from the Latin *exempli gratias* and it means, literally, *for example.* Periods come after each letter and a comma normally follows:

Any facial response (e.g., a surprised blink of both eyes) was recorded.

The abbreviation *i.e.* is from the Latin *id est,* meaning *that is.* Loosely, *i.e.* is used to mean *therefore* or *in other words.* Periods come after each letter and a comma follows:

In every case Angle 1 was greater than Angle 2; i.e., every viewer perceived a circle.

The phrase *et al.*—from the Latin *et alii,* which means *and others*—must always be typed with a space between the "t" and the "a" and with a period after the "l":

Schweiger et al. applied the neural network method.

Never begin a sentence with any of these abbreviations; if you want to begin a sentence with "for example," or "therefore," write the words out.

etc.

According to many professors, *etc.* should not be used in formal scientific writing because it is nonspecific. It means, literally, *and other things.* Tacking on *etc.* at the end of a list introduced by "for example" or "such as" is a bit sloppy, because "for example" suggests that you have carefully selected some key examples, which the *etc.* then undermines. Good alternatives to etc. are "for example" or "such as" followed by just a few concrete representative examples that best demonstrate your point.

Fact/Factor

Use *fact* only in reference to *matters capable of direct verification;* do not use it in matters of subjective judgment:

> The fact is that the output of many oil wells is a mixture of both oil and salt water.

Use *factor* literally to describe a relationship in which *one thing is an actual agent for another thing:*

> Porosity and permeability are factors in the level of groundwater pollution.

Generally acceptable synonyms for *factor* are "element," "ingredient," and "component."

Farther/Further

Strictly speaking, *farther* is a word describing *matters of distance,* while *further* is used in a more *general* fashion to cover all other situations:

> Long Island is farther away from Cape Charles than Cape May.

> Antarctica must be explored further.

> She is further along in her schooling than I.

Fewer/Less

Both are adjectives, but *fewer* is usually used to describe *countable nouns* while *less* is used to describe *noncountable nouns.* Countable nouns are often physical whereas noncountable ones are often nonphysical:

The industrial trend is in the direction of more machines and fewer people. ("People" are countable.)

There was less noise during the accident than one would have expected. ("Noise" is noncountable.)

However, sentences involving *periods of time, sums of money,* or *specific measurements* usually require *less:*

It was lowered less than 50 feet.

The procedure took less than two weeks.

Imply/Infer

These two words are too often used interchangeably, but they are completely different in meaning. *Imply* means *to suggest* or *to indicate; infer* involves *a person actively applying deduction to a situation:*

Water droplets accumulating on the outside of a cold glass of water can imply a hot humid day.

We can infer that Stonehenge was an early calendar.

In terms of

These words are virtually meaningless and are almost never needed. We tend to fall back on them because we hear them so often on the news and in speeches. (Dan Quayle's public response to Murphy Brown's single-parent status was "Illegitimacy is something that we should talk about only in terms of not having it.") The words may sound impressive at first, but *in terms of* is really just a wordy and sloppy transition. Usually it is an unoriginal disguise for a simple preposition, such as *in,* or the phrase is not needed at all, or it is an indication that a sentence should be simplified. "In terms of the cost, it is high," is easily revised to "Its cost is high." Do not use *in terms of,* or do so trembling.

Irregardless

It is just wrong—an invented word. Use *regardless.*

It's/Its

These two words probably represent the most common usage problem in papers, but the distinction between the words is simple. *It's* always means *it is. Its* never does. If we look closely, there seems to be an inherent inconsistency, because we usually use apostrophes to indicate possession, but certain words, for instance *his* and *its,* automatically show possession and need no apostrophes. If you write *it's* be sure that you mean *two words* rather than one. Read it to yourself aloud if you have to, reading every *it's* as *it is.* If you do this, you will get it right.

Similarly, the following words automatically show possession and therefore never need possessive apostrophes: *theirs, ours, yours, hers.*

Lay/Lie

Lay implies an agent acting on something, and it means *to put, place,* or *prepare.* Its forms are *laying, laid* (past tense), and *laid* (with "has," "have," or "had"):

They were laid there centuries ago. (Past tense—they were placed.)

Lie means *to recline or to be situated,* and its forms are *lying, lay* (past tense), and *lain* (with "has," "have," or "had"):

It lay undisturbed for thousands of years. (Past tense—it was *situated.*)

Lead/Led

Lead is a present-tense verb meaning *to guide or direct. Led* is the *past tense* of the same verb, and must not be spelled with an "a":

She led a discussion on how to lead the group.

May/Might

May expresses *possibility* or *permission. Might* is used in the same way, but implies *less certainty* than *may:*

This outcrop may be studied. (Implies that permission has been give.)

This outcrop might be studied. (Implies that the possibility merely exists.)

One/You

It is a shame that many high school teachers continue to do things such as penalize students five points for each occurrence of *you* or *one* in an essay. You are permitted to use these words in writing, but you must do so sparingly, appropriately, and literally. *You* and *your* are informal and directed explicitly at the reader; thus they are appropriate for *memos, letters,* or *a set of instructions* designed to apply to the reader in the act of reading:

I am responding to the memo you wrote to me on March 20.

Your first task is to remove the nozzle.

In more formal, technical documents, rely on the word *one* to refer to *people* generally, ideally as you present them as potential *thinkers* or *doers:*

One can assume that there is a threshold axis above which the eyes simply can not detect the difference between a circle and an ellipse.

Finally, be careful not to switch back and forth arbitrarily between *you* and *one;* be consistent and use your common sense.

Per

Literally, *per* means *for every or according to:*

It costs 30 cents per gallon.

Per your instructions, I completed the lab.

The phrase "as per" is incorrect—a redundancy.

Percent/Percentage

These two terms are not interchangeable. Percent means *per hundred* and can either be written out or expressed by the symbol %:

The maximum error that can be introduced by over-mixing is 10 %.

Percentage is used to refer to a *general relationship* rather than a specific measure:

A large percentage of the people voted, but only 20 percent of the votes have been counted.

Pretty/Quite/Rather/Very

In technical writing, avoid the words *very, pretty, quite,* and *rather* as adjectives. They are too nonspecific for your needs, and many professors are sensitive to their use. Other terms such as "virtually," "highly," "essentially," or "relatively," may work in their place, but be certain to use these terms literally and sparingly. *Rather* is, of course, valid in an "a rather than b" construction.

Principal/Principle

Principal means *first, primary,* or *main:*

The principal feldspar is orthoclase.

A *principle* is a *doctrine,* a *truth:*

We discussed the principle of differential entrapment of petroleum.

Respective/Respectively

Respective is an adjective, usually meaning *particular:*

On a References page, article titles appear after their respective authors.

Respectively means *in the order mentioned:*

Aluminum and iron are evident in about 8 percent and 5 percent, respectively, of the earth's crust.

s / 's

When you add an *s* to an acronym or a number you are simply pluralizing it and there is no need to put an apostrophe in front of it. Therefore, *SSTs* (sea surface temperatures) is more acceptable than *SST's*. Use the apostrophe before the *s* with an acronym or a number only to show possession (i.e., *an 1860's law*).

That/Which

The rules governing these two words are a bit flexible, but *which* is too often used where *that* should be. *That* is preferable when you are *defining or restricting a noun:*

A law that does not have public support cannot be enforced. ("A law that" helps to limit the meaning to just one kind of law.)

New Orleans is built on unconsolidated sediments that tend to become compacted naturally. ("Sediments that" helps to define particular kinds of sediments.)

The following line from a nursery rhyme is instructive here, because all of the *thats* are correct:

This is the rat that ate the cat that lived in the house that Jack built.

In contrast, *which* introduces a phrase that provides *descriptive yet incidental information,* and *which* usually requires commas on one or both ends of the phrase it introduces:

The law, which was enacted in 1897, was soon challenged by the courts.

Approximately 71 percent of the earth's surface is covered by a world-wide body of sea water, which is interconnected.

In a loose sense, you use *that* to *complete a noun* and *which* simply to *describe a noun.*

Try and

Wrong, but often used. *Try to* is correct:

They will try to solve the problem.

Chapter 5

Equations, Figures, and Tables

> *The grand aim of all science is to cover the greatest number of empirical facts by logical deduction from the smallest number of hypotheses or axioms.*
> —Albert Einstein

Equations, figures, and tables are great opportunities to present your ideas, explanations, and experimental results in a form that is professional, aesthetic, and—tell the truth—even *fun*. The computer has truly revolutionized the typing of equations and the presentation of graphics for us. However, some professors long for the days when figures had to be drawn laboriously by hand, because the cost and the labor made it inviting to keep figures and tables to a minimum. Now, graphic overkill is common, especially by graduate students; some professors call it the *USA Today* mentality. We must keep in mind that graphics are a means to an end, not an end in themselves.

Also, since readers might leap right to a table or figure while reading an article, it is vital that each table or figure is meaningfully presented and works both independently and as part of the text. Presenting figures and tables well is a worthwhile art that takes years to develop, which is part of the reason why you should make the process as simple as possible for both you and your readers. Carefully study the tables and figures published in the best journals in your field, and apply the same conventions of presentation to your own work.

This chapter's aim is not to make it easier for you to create equations, figures, or tables—computers have made their creation easy enough—but to teach you how to make your presentation of them professional. For much more on how to present tables and figures, and for a nifty review of the different types, I highly recommend Paul V. Anderson's *Technical Writing: A Reader-Centered Approach*. I have looked at over 40 textbooks that give space to the subject, and Anderson's chapters are the best I have seen. The book is in most college and university libraries and available through bookstores.

Equations

This section offers concrete advice about some of the mechanics of style for presenting equations. For specific rules about such details as punctuation, spacing, or the flushing of elements, the best idea is to check out a journal or textbook in your field and learn by example. In addition, the following advice will help you to integrate equations into your sentences and understand them as grammatical units.

Style for Equations

- Grammatically, you can think of an equation as a single noun and generally treat it as such. Usually an equation is followed by a comma after it is presented, especially if you also follow the equation with descriptions of its individual members.

- Short and uncomplicated equations can simply be included as part of a sentence without any special spacing. However, be sure that the equation flows as a readable unit of the sentence. Never expect an equation by itself to be a complete sentence.

- Set off and *center* equations on their own separate lines of text if the equations are long, contain more than one or two symbols that must be identified, or contain members such as subscripted numbers or expressions with numerators or denominators that fall on different lines.

- When you center an equation, skip at least one line above and below it, and skip an extra line or two if the equation includes any symbols of more than letter height. Make the equation easy to find and easy to read.

- If an equation is too long for a single line, break the equation just before a "verb" (such as the = sign) or a "conjunction" (such as the + sign) and make the symbol the first member of the next line, then continue the equation.

- When appropriate, define members of the equation just after you present it, usually by introducing them with the word "where." For example, if you wanted to define "t" and "n" just after they appeared in an equation, a phrase such as this would appear: "where t is the film thickness and n is a constant equal to 0.4."

- When appropriate, define any symbols that you use.

- It is common and handy to use the word "we" to introduce equations to enhance efficiency, foster readability, and promote the active voice. For example: "We can express the distance of this transition region by the equation . . . ." Handy phrases with which to introduce equations include "we can express," "we can approximate," and "we can describe."

- If possible, do not let an equation spill from one page to another.

- Equations are not normally numbered, but if you need to refer to any equations elsewhere in the text then you may wish to number all equations in sequence. Do this by identifying the number of the equation in parentheses at the right-hand margin of the line where the equation appears. Then it becomes a simple matter for both you and the reader to locate this equation when you refer to it with a phrase such as "Equation 3 describes a contrasting relationship." If you number an equation, be sure the number is set far enough away from it that it does not seem to be a member of the equation.

Sample Equation

The sample equation that follows is excerpted from the *Bureau of Mines Style Guide* (1). Note how the equation is followed by a comma and is presented as a grammatical member of a smooth, simple, flowing sentence. Note also the use of semicolons and commas to separate members of the equation as each is described.

The duration of the heating cycle can be approximated by the equation

$$t = 2R_tC_t,$$

where t = cycle time, s; R_t = resistance, Ω; and C_t = capacitance, F.

Figures and Tables

Because figures and tables can now be created at the mere click of a few keys, it is tempting to swamp the reader with them or get caught up so much in their fanciness that some fundamentals are ignored. Some papers include three-dimensional pie charts that are misleading because of the dimensions created by the 3-D effect, beautifully colored bar graphs or maps with the different colors all representing the same thing, and fancy fonts and special effects that dazzle the eye but have no other function in the graphic. Just as commonly, there is a lack of elemental detail or care: Xeroxed figures or tables from a textbook with the original (and therefore inaccurate) page numbers not even whited out; a figure whose caption is simply "Costs"; undefined terms, unlabeled axes, uncited data. The list could go on for too long.

Yet these errors are just as easily avoided as committed, especially if you make a habit of only using figures and tables when it is appropriate to do so. Tables and figures are supposed to be designed to simplify and condense the presentation of what is otherwise complex information. Their function is to save the reader time, enhance comprehension, and allow rapid comparison and interpretation of relationships or trends. Remember this as you prepare figures and tables, and act accordingly.

Textual References to Figures and Tables

- Number figures and tables consecutively in the text, beginning with the number 1. Be sure to number figures and tables separately from each other.

- Capitalize the "t" in "table" and the "f" in "figure" when you refer to a specific table or figure created in your text. (Some journals do not follow this convention, but most do.)

- "Table 3 and 4" is incorrect because each table is a separate entity. If you refer to more than one table or figure at a time, pluralize the reference. "Tables 3 and 4" is correct.

- Introduce figures and tables in your text in logical places and in logical ways. In some cases, it may simply be appropriate to write "see Figure 7" in parentheses at the end of a paragraph that prepared the reader to view the figure; in other cases, it is appropriate to introduce a figure or table at the beginning of the paragraph and build the entire paragraph around it.

- In your body text, always spell out the point that you want your reader to get from your figure or table. Example:

  As Figure 8 indicates, the modulus of the transverse direction was always equal to or greater than the modulus of the machine direction.

- If possible, use some of your body text to interpret a table or figure, but only to a sensible degree, and usually *after* it is presented rather than before. Avoid redundancy. If your pie chart shows percentages for the market distribution of platinum, there is no point in your repeating these percentages in your body text unless you interpret them.

- When a reference to a table or a figure is a sentence subject, match it with an interpretive verb to describe how the figure or table works. Examples:

  Figure 2 illustrates the predominant orientation of acicular particles in magnetic storage material.

  Figure 5 compares two magnetization curves for hard and soft magnetic materials.

- "Show" is generally a safe verb to use to describe a table or figure, but beware of overusing it or using it too loosely. Good alternatives to "show" include "display," "demonstrate," "illustrate," "depict" (for figures), and "list" (for tables). As always, search for the best verb to describe your figure or table.

Aesthetics for Figures and Tables

- Do not crowd a table or figure, neither within itself nor within your text. Give it room to breathe. When it appears among your body text, skip several lines above and below it.

- Do not clutter any visual information with needless items or parts. Always beware of creating a 3-D or special effects monster. Everything in the table or figure should have a function—therefore do not do things such as number items unless the numbers actually mean something.

- Organize information so that it is prioritized and easily seen. It is acceptable to do something such as boldface a part of a picture or a column of a table to emphasize it, but be certain to explain the emphasis in the caption.

- Unless instructed otherwise, as a general rule you should place figures and tables right in the text as soon as possible after they are mentioned. If the figure or table can not be imbedded into the body text, it is common to put it on a separate numbered page that appears on the page immediately following the first body text reference. It is also generally acceptable to include all tables and figures, in order, on separate pages at the end of the document just after the References page.

- Give each table and figure its own separate page unless it is logical to group them.

- If it can be avoided, no single figure or table should spill over to a second page. To keep this from happening, you may orient the table of figure sideways or break it into parts.

Captions for Figures and Tables

- The caption for a *figure* appears *below* the graphic; for a *table, above.* It is easy to get this wrong accidentally.

- If possible, boldface or underscore the word "figure" or "table" and the number in the caption, then present the caption in plain text with the first letters of important words capitalized.

- Always concentrate on completeness and concreteness as you caption figures and tables. "Figure 3: Air Flow" is far less illuminating and accurate than the following:

Figure 3: The Motion Of A Parcel Of Air As It Flows Across A Mountain.

- Do not be afraid to have lengthy figure and table captions—better that than confusing or incomplete ones. Write the caption so that it would make sense even if the table or figure were ripped from the paper.

- If your figure or table is essentially the same as or based on another author's, but you recreated or adapted it, it is standard to include the words "Adapted from" followed by the author's name somewhere in the caption.

- Always cite the figure or table as you present it if it—or its data—came from a source, using the same citation style that you have used throughout the paper. The most logical place for the citation to appear is usually at the end of the caption.

Fundamentals for Figures

- Be sure to name figures properly; do not accidentally call them tables. Figures are *drawn or photographed pictures.*

- As a general rule, orient figures from left to right.

- Use line graphs to plot *continuous variables* such as time or temperature.

- Use pie charts or bar graphs to depict *discontinuous variables* such as percentages or sampling that occurred in intervals.

- Use photographs or drawings for inherently visually-oriented material such as a cloud or a camshaft.

- Use flowcharts to represent pathways of activities and outcomes.

- If possible, label the axes of graphs with full words: "temperature versus time" rather than "T versus t."

- Be certain that your legend—that part of the figure where you define any symbols or other visual markers that appear—is readable, clear, and meaningfully placed. As long as it does not overwhelm the rest of the figure, do not be afraid to make the legend large.

- Use footnotes (a simple asterisk to indicate them will do) for explanatory material such as the number of respondents to a survey or the fact that certain values were estimated.

Fundamentals for Tables

- Be sure to name tables properly; do not accidentally call them figures. Tables are *lists of numbers and words.*

- Make certain that each entry in the left-most column (called the stub) applies across its entire row, and that each column heading pertains to all entries beneath it.

- Arrange stub items logically—largest to smallest, alphabetically, by category, or for emphasis.

- Straight lines are often used to separate the table's title from the column heads, the column heads from the body of the table, and the bottom of the table from the paper's text or the table's footnotes. Boxes around and within the table are also appropriate.

- If possible, construct a table so that the reader's eye can primarily travel down a column rather than have to read along a row.

- Use footnotes (a simple asterisk to indicate them will do) for explanatory material such as the number of respondents to a survey or the fact that certain values were estimated.

Sample Figure

The figure that follows appeared in the background section of a senior thesis by Shana Gordon, a geosciences student at Penn State. The figure is meaningful because the reader must understand what it depicts—the deposition of bituminous coals—in order to grasp the nature of the testing that will be discussed later in the thesis. Note also how an entire paragraph of the body text is devoted to explaining the figure.

As water pushes inland during a transgression, a sequence of under-clay (furthest inland), coal, and shale (furthest seaward) is deposited, as shown in Figure 1. After the maximum transgressive stage the coast-line regresses seaward, with the coal forming a "V" around the open water sediments. The back swamp clay is deposited above the coal in regressive sequences; the underclay is an open water sediment.

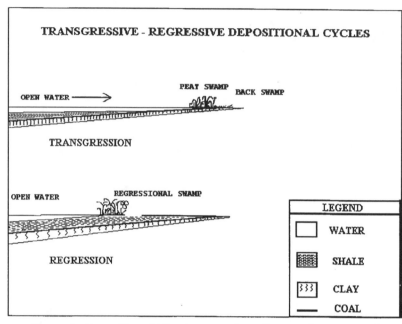

Figure 1. Deposition of bituminous coals as it occurs in transgressive-regressive cycles.

Sample Table

The table that follows is excerpted from the same thesis as the sample figure. Note the specificity of the table caption, which is also cited because some of the table data were provided by a source. Also note the level of discussion following the table's presentation, and how the writer uses the data from the table to move toward an explanation of the trends that the table reveals.

The results of borehole dilution testing and slug testing on wells B2, B3, and B4 are summarized in Table 4. The hydraulic conductivities computed from the borehole dilution test velocities for wells B2, B3, and B4 range over an order of magnitude, a reasonable spread for hydraulic properties of close, but varying, test sites.

Table 4. Water velocities and hydraulic conductivities of the Lower Kittanning coal at the Kaufmann site in Clearfield County, Pennsylvania, from slug tests in November 1991 and borehole dilution (BD) tests November 1992 (Abate, personal correspondence, 1992).

	Velocity - BD tests	Hydraulic Conductivity - BD tests ($p_e = 0.01$)	Hydraulic Conductivity- BD tests ($p_e = 0.05$)	Hydraulic Conductivity - slug tests
B2	0.054 ft/d	1.1×10^{-2} ft/d	0.054 ft/d	0.19 ft/d
B3	0.32 ft/d	0.07 ft/d	0.32 ft/d	8.9×10^{-3} ft/d
B4	0.06 ft/d	1.2×10^{-2} ft/d	6.0×10^{-2} ft/d	2.8×10^{-2} ft/d

The hydraulic conductivities computed from the borehole dilution test velocities are significantly lower than those predicted by Huang and Sheltons' core analysis of Middle Kittanning coal (see section 2.1.3.). As shown on Table 4, the borehole dilution hydraulic conductivity values for wells B2 and B4 agree reasonably well with their corresponding slug test values, assuming an effective porosity between 0.01 and 0.05. This effective porosity seems high, but the dip of bedding in the study area is opposite the regional dip. This implies slumping, which could increase the effective porosity significantly.

Using Sources

Chapter 6

It has yet to be proved that intelligence has any survival value.

—Arthur C. Clarke

This chapter helps you to attack the most common problems writers have as they document their sources. It is both normal yet frustrating to do battle with the problem of properly documenting sources (telling where your information came from) in your papers. Even seasoned writers struggle with this.

We will start with the most obvious problem: plagiarism. Outright plagiarism is a serious offense, and, when professors forgive it, it is usually because they see it as a terribly dumb and desperate act. In a composition class that I taught, I once had a student plagiarize from someone in the same section, and in the hallways I have heard students brag to each other about getting away with blatant plagiarism on papers.

Nevertheless, as a writing tutor who discusses this issue almost daily, I am convinced that many students plagiarize accidentally—either because they simply are not sure when to document their sources or because they do not want it to appear that most of the paper's material came from sources. The simple truth is that, in many cases, as much as 70 or 80 percent of a paper's text should and will be directly based on your research, and there is nothing wrong with that as long as you use and document your sources properly. After all, most of your assignments are probably *research* papers, and part of the research process is for you to let your sources shape your thinking about a topic. The ideal is to read all of your sources, highlight or otherwise take down notes from them, write a detailed outline, then write out a first draft, working in the best information from your sources as you go and giving your own personal spin to the ideas wherever appropriate. Then revise and revise and revise.

But I realize that this rarely happens. In fact, the norm for many students is that they spend a week or so Xeroxing anything that looks relevant in the library, then, 24 or 12 hours before the deadline, they sit down and start tapping madly into the word processor, sometimes simply lifting whole paragraphs from their sources and hoping that it looks like their own work, loudly assuring themselves and their friends that they "work best under pressure." If this is your technique you will certainly run into trouble, and you will find that it fails you miserably when it comes to writing a thesis or working on a lengthy writing project on the job. Writing a long research paper in a day is a bit like pulling an all-nighter on Christmas Eve to crochet a quilt—you will find that the end product looks hurried and flimsy, and you can be sure that you have left many loose ends and produced a lousy Christmas gift.

Whatever your writing process, even if you are in the habit of resorting to the patch and pray method, the material in this chapter will help you to use sources more correctly. I review when, how, and why sources should be cited, provide a sample paragraph with the sources properly documented, and suggest four concrete ways that you can plant your sources within your own assertions. I also review the two methods that students in science and engineering are typically expected to use when they cite sources, and you must be sure to use the correct one for your discipline.

Fundamentals of Using Sources

A colleague of mine once told me a story that proves how small the academic world can be while underscoring the best reason to document sources: Doing so can only make you friends; failing to do so can only make you enemies. This colleague was asked to review a proposal submitted to the National Science Foundation, and was irate when he realized that an author of the proposal did not acknowledge my colleague's work when he clearly should have. An investigation confirmed my colleague's suspicions, which stung all the more because he had once actually nominated the author for an award. For my colleague, the author, and the National Science Foundation, this became an unpleasant situation all around, breeding distrust and embarrassment. A lot of time was wasted. All of this could have been avoided if the author had merely put his research into the appropriate context by properly acknowledging his sources. Instead, the author—whether intentionally or not—plagiarized.

When you write papers, you might be tempted to plagiarize to try to cover up the fact that almost all of your paper came directly from sources. Your well-read professors will not be fooled by this tactic, though, and part of your job as a researcher and writer is to organize, assimilate, and recast your information in your own form. If you find yourself doing such things as using the same source for several paragraphs in a row or failing even to provide your own topic sentences for paragraphs, you are obviously not doing your job as a thinking writer. Do not fall back on the flimsy excuse that you might as well just copy it exactly as it appeared because you see no way to phrase it any better than the original author did. The context for your writing is different from the context of the original. The reason you use sources in the first place is to simplify and summarize information and weave it into the pattern of your own ideas, and your pattern of ideas will develop as you write and do your research.

Also, you must remember that the type of writing you do rarely relies on direct quotations, because the author's exact wording is generally not as relevant as the data reported. In a technical paper on mine safety, for example, direct quotation of these sentences is probably inappropriate: "Since 1870, 121,000 mining deaths have occurred; 1.7 million lost-time injuries have been recorded since 1930. All of this has contributed to the public's negative perception of mining and the NIMBY mentality." There is probably no good reason to quote these sentences directly, especially because some of the material is data and some is interpretation. The exact wording does not matter, but some of the material does, so the writer's job is to extract only the relevant information, use it, and cite the source. Similarly, there is no good reason to quote this sentence directly: "Acid mine drainage has been and continues to be a major problem generated by the mining of coal in Pennsylvania and elsewhere in the world." In this instance, the information is *so general* that it need not even be cited, but neither should the sentence itself just be lifted out and plopped into your paper. Ideally, the information from the above sentence would simply end up as an inherent part of a sentence of your own creation such as this one: "This paper explores the three chief reasons why acid mine drainage continues to be a major environmental problem in Pennsylvania."

In sum then, follow these fundamental rules as you use sources:

- Summarize and simplify the most relevant information from your sources.

- Let your research influence—but not control entirely—your thinking and writing process.

- Integrate your sources efficiently within the context of your own work.

- When appropriate, document your sources.

Information that always must be cited includes:

- Quotations, opinions, and predictions—whether directly quoted or paraphrased.

- Statistics derived by the original author.

- Visuals in the original.

- Another author's theories.

- Case studies.

- Another author's direct experimental methods or results.

When Sources Must *Be Cited*

- Another author's unique research procedures or findings.

If you use specific information of the type just mentioned, document it; otherwise you could be plagiarizing. Better safe than lazy. By citing the source of your information you point to an authority rather than ask your reader to trust your memory or what might appear to be your own idea. Even though you *can* recall a statistic or a description of a process, for example, citation of such information—if it truly came directly from a source—gives more credibility to your writing and assures both you and your reader of the accuracy, timeliness, and even the potential bias or limitedness of your information. You *know* whether or not you looked at a source to get the information originally, and so does your intelligent reader. It is your job to take careful notes from your sources as you review them and document your sources accurately so that they provide underpinnings for your overall work. If possible, track down the original sources rather than repeat another author's interpretation second-hand, and only cite sources that you have actually read and used. Be honest, smart, and safe.

Integrating Your Sources

This section details ways for you to integrate your sources into your own work. It is easy to feel at times that you have done so much research that you are simply spitting back various ideas that others formulated. That is why it is important for you to develop your own assertions where possible, organize your findings in such a way that your ideas are still the thrust of the paper, and take care not to rely too much on any one source, or you will find that your paper's content is controlled too heavily by that source.

In practical terms, some ways to develop and back up your assertions include:

- Organize your sources before and as you write so that they BLEND, even within paragraphs. Your paper—on both the overall level and the paragraph level—should reveal relationships among your sources, and should also reveal the relationships between your own ideas and those of your sources.

- As much as is practical, make the paper's INTRODUCTION and CONCLUSION your own ideas or your own synthesis of the ideas inherent in your research. Use sources *minimally* in your introduction and conclusion.

- In general, use the OPENINGS AND CLOSINGS OF YOUR PARAGRAPHS to reveal your work—"enclose" your sources among your assertions. At a minimum, make your own topic sentences and wrap-up sentences for paragraphs.

- When appropriate, practice such RHETORICAL STRATEGIES as analysis, synthesis, comparison, contrast, summary, description, definition, evaluation, hypothesis, generalization, classification, hierarchical structure, and even narration. Prove to your reader that you are *thinking* as you write.

Another vital practice is making it clear exactly where your own ideas end and the cited information begins. It is your job to help your reader draw the line between these two things, often by the way you word the opening part of your cited information. A phrase such as "A 1979 study revealed that" is an obvious announcement of documentation to come. Another recommended technique is the insertion of the author's name right into the text to announce the beginning of your cited information. You may worry that you are not allowed to give the actual names of the researchers you have studied in the paper's text, but just the opposite is true. In fact, the more respectable an author you cite, the more impressed your reader will be with your material while reading. If you note that the source is NASA or Carl Sagan or *The Wall Street Journal* right in your text, it will have a more profound effect on the readers than if you make them guess or flip to the References page to look up the source.

What follows is an excerpt from a political science paper that simply and admirably draws the line between writer and cited information:

> The above political upheaval illuminates the reasons behind the growing Iranian hatred of foreign interference; as a result of this hatred, three enduring geopolitical patterns have evolved in Iran, as noted by John Limbert. First…

Note how the writer begins by redefining her previous paragraph's topic (political upheaval), then connects this to Iran's hatred of foreign interference, then suggests a causal relationship and ties everything into John Limbert's analysis—thereby announcing that a synthesis of Limbert's work is coming. This writer's work also becomes more credible and meaningful because, right in the text, she announces the name of a person who is a recognized authority in the field. Even in this short excerpt, it is obvious that this writer is using proper documentation and backing up her own assertions with confidence and style.

Writing a paragraph with the sources properly cited can seem a tricky task at first, but the process is straightforward enough, especially when we analyze an example. Writing and documenting a paragraph is really just a matter of thinking clearly about a topic you have researched and transferring that thinking to the page. To illustrate, a tidy sample paragraph follows, with the sources properly documented in the author-year system, Next, the genesis of the paragraph is analyzed through the author's eyes.

> The millions of species of plants and animals on the earth have a phenomenal influence on the human species. Not only do they provide a substantial amount of our food, they are of great value in medicine and

Anatomy of a Well-Documented Paragraph

science. Over 60 percent of the purchases we make at the pharmacy contain substances that are derived from wild organisms (Myers 1988). Studies of plants and animals have led to discoveries in virtually all of the sciences, from biology and chemistry to psychology and astronomy (Wilson 1991). Furthermore, plants and animals are vital to the maintenance of our ecosystem. Their diversity and balance directly control food webs, nutrient diversity, supplies of fresh water, climate consistency, and waste disposal (Ehrlich 1988). Finally, many species act as barometers of our environment. The salmon, for example, is extremely sensitive to changes in the condition of the water in which it lives. Any abnormality in population or behavior of fish usually indicates some type of chemical imbalance in the water. The same is true of butterflies and their relationship with prominent agricultural areas. Clearly, the millions of species of plants and animals in the world are vital to the continued thriving of the human population.

Now let us walk through the paragraph and its use of sources. The first two sentences of the paragraph assert the author's personal view about the value of the world's species (a view shaped by his research, no doubt), which he is about to back up by using three recent sources. Next, the author cited a source (Myers) which had included a statistic ("over 60 percent of the purchases we make at the pharmacy"). Without this source cited, the reader could easily believe that the author estimated loosely or simply relied on his memory for the statistic. The next source cited (Wilson) involved a sweeping and general claim that the author of the above paragraph derived from a textbook he had read. The author was at first not sure whether to cite the source, but he wisely decided that he should because he realized that he had in fact had Wilson's book open to a particular page and referred to it as he wrote the sentence. The next source (Ehrlich) was cited because the author had gone through a whole chapter of Ehrlich's book in order to write the sentence, usually using Ehrlich's exact section headings from the chapter as the sentence material. The final examples of the salmon and the butterfly were based directly on the author's personal experience of working at a fish hatchery for a summer, so documenting sources was not an issue. The fact that the author found a way to tie this experiential knowledge in with his research is testimony to the fact that he was thinking as he wrote the paragraph. He allowed his sources to blend with each other, but he did not allow them to do the thinking for him. More evidence of the author's control over his material is his mid-paragraph transition sentence (beginning with "Furthermore"), his labeling of species as "barometers" of the environment a few sentences later, and his closing sentence, which wraps up the paragraph's ideas neatly by making a general affirmative and confident statement.

Not every paragraph should look exactly like this, of course, but every paragraph should be written with the same kind of care about how, when, and why the sources are documented.

The Author-Year System of Documentation

In science and engineering, the author-year system of documentation is used more on the undergraduate level than the graduate. Fields that have ties to the liberal arts, such as geography, human development, and political science, tend to favor the author-year system.

Your basic job when using this system is to indicate right in the text—in parentheses—the author(s) and year of publication of the reference you are citing. Since the citation becomes part of your sentence, you delay the appropriate punctuation until after the parentheses.

Sample Author-Year Citations

In the following example, both the author and year are given in parentheses:

> In recent decades, anthropogenic activities such as deforestation, desertification, and urbanization have significantly altered the land surface (Nicholson 1987).

Many writers identify the source as soon as they begin the reference, including the author's name directly in the text and supplying only the year in parentheses:

> Decker et al. (1981) estimated that the Mt. St. Helens eruption…

If you use two or more articles written by the same author(s) in the same year, you distinguish between the documents in your text and on your References page by using an "a,b,c" system, providing an identifying letter after the year:

> Toon (1989a) found evidence of . . .

If no author's name is given in the original, the publication's name or the publisher's name (or a clear shortened form of it) should suffice. In the following example, a document authored by a governmental agency (which would be fully referenced on a References page) is identified by a shortened form of its name:

> Coordinated measurements planned in the framework of the original program should help to explain the apparent discrepancies in the data (PRIMO document, 1989).

Style For The References Page—Author-Year System

You enable your reader to locate the original sources of your documented information by using a separate References page at the end of your text. You could, of course, choose any respected magazine or journal in your field as a model for your References page, and this is often the easiest path to take.

As a general rule, on your References page you provide the following information in the following order:

- The names and initials of all authors, beginning with the last name of the first author listed, followed by a comma.

- Year of publication, followed by a colon.

- Title of the document or article being cited, with the key words capitalized. Quotation marks could be used around article titles.

- Title of book, magazine, or journal, underlined or italicized, with journal titles abbreviated.

- Publication information—if citing a BOOK or PRIVATELY PUBLISHED DOCUMENT, provide the publisher's name and location, then the total number of pages, separated by commas; if citing a JOURNAL or MAGAZINE, provide the volume number in boldface, then a comma, then the page numbers of the article being cited.

Special References Page Dilemmas

Especially when you are referring to things such as government documents, statistical reports, and unsigned magazine articles, exact authorship can seem a difficult thing to determine. In brief, publications of an organization are considered to be authored by that organization. If no author's name is identified, do not use the word "Anonymous" as the author's name; instead, if the U.S. Department of Commerce or the name of a company is the only author identified on the publication, consider that organization to be the author. If you interviewed or received written correspondence as part of your research, list the person's name, affiliation, and any relevant dates. Remember that the general rule is to provide enough information so that your readers can obtain copies of your references if they wish. Where appropriate, you might even provide a mailing address.

Sample References Page—Author-Year System

In the author-year system, your references are listed on a separate References page in alphabetical order, using the last names of the authors. The type should be double spaced, lines should not be skipped between each reference, and a hanging indent of five spaces should be used after the first line of each reference.

Always include the word "References," boldfaced if possible, in the center at the top of the page. An example follows:

REFERENCES

Charlock, T.P., and V. Ramanathan, 1985: The Albedo Field and Cloud Radiative Forcing Produced by a General Circulation Model with Internally Generated Cloud Optics. *J. Atmos. Sci.*, 42, 1408-1429.

Ozick, B., 1987: The Physical Oceanography of the Mediterranean
    Sea, Bell Publishing Co. Austin, TX, 176 pp.
PRIMO document, 1989: Preparatory document on the development of
    PRIMO, an international research program in the western
    Mediterranean. Published by PRIMO, Inc., Paris, 29 pp.

Generally, the number system is favored in fields where you typically report experimental work that was completed in a laboratory. Technical fields such as materials science, aerospace engineering, and biology tend to favor the number system.

When you use the Number system, your basic job is to indicate in your text—either in parentheses or brackets—a number that corresponds to a source on your References page. The first source you cite in your text receives the number 1, the second number 2, and so on. If you repeat a reference to a source later in the text, it retains its *original* number: thus all references to source number 4 will receive a 4 after them in parentheses or brackets. You delay the appropriate punctuation until *after* the parentheses or brackets.

Sample Number System Citations

What follows is a typical example of the use of the number system:

If the load on the thrust bearing can be decreased by some means, the life of the turbodrill can be significantly increased (1).

Many authors prefer to identify the source at the beginning of the reference, perhaps including the author's name directly in the text:

Gould et al. (5) found a clear relation between. . .

The number system is especially handy for citing equations, because you can simply insert the citation number logically as you introduce the equation to avoid confusion with any other numbers:

The line's slope is used in the following equation (7) to calculate…

Style For The References Page—Number System

You enable your reader to locate the original sources of your documented information by using a separate References page at the end of your text. You could simply choose a respected journal in your field and use this as a model for your References page.

As a general rule, on your References page you provide the following information in the following order:

- The number of the reference, followed by a period.

- The initials and last names of all authors, followed by a comma.

The Number System of Documentation

- Title of the article enclosed in quotation marks, followed by a comma.

- Title of book, magazine, or journal, underlined or italicized, with journal titles abbreviated.

- Volume numbers or editors—if citing a JOURNAL or MAGAZINE, provide the volume number in boldface, followed by the issue number in brackets; if citing a BOOK with editors or volume numbers, provide the names of the editors or the volume numbers.

- Publication information—if citing a BOOK or PRIVATELY PUBLISHED DOCUMENT, provide the relevant page numbers, then the publisher's name and location (all separated by commas), then the year, followed by a period; if citing a JOURNAL or MAGAZINE, provide the relevant page numbers of the article being cited, then the year in parentheses, followed by a period.

Special References Page Dilemmas

Especially when you are referring to things such as government documents, statistical reports, and unsigned magazine articles, exact authorship can seem a difficult thing to determine. In brief, publications of an organization are considered to be authored by that organization. If no author's name is identified, do not use the word "Anonymous" as the author's name; instead, if the National Research Council of Canada or the name of a company is the only author identified on the publication, consider that organization to be the author. Remember that the general rule is to provide enough information so that your readers can obtain copies of your references if they wish. Where appropriate, you might even provide a mailing address.

Sample References Page—Number System

In the Number system your references are listed on a separate References page in the order in which they were cited by first appearance in your text, and they are numbered accordingly. Each source is, of course, simply listed once, even though it may have been referred to in the text numerous times. The type should be double spaced, lines should not be skipped between each reference, and a hanging indent of five spaces should be used after the first line of each reference. Always include the word "References," boldfaced if possible, in the center at the top of the page. An example follows:

REFERENCES

1. M. Poulain and J. Lucas, "Optical Properties of Zirconium Tetrafluoride-Based Glasses," *Mater. Res. Bull.* **10**, 243 (1975).

2. G. E. Rindone, "Influence of Platinum Nucleation on the Crystallization of Lithium Silicate Glasses," *J. Am. Ceram. Soc.*, **41** [1] 41-42 (1958).

3. I. Gutzow and S. Toschev, "The Kinetics of Nucleation and the Formation of Glass Ceramics," in *Advances in Nucleation and Crystallization of Glasses*, pp. 10-23, Edited by L.L. Hench and S.W. Frieman. American Ceramic Society, Columbus, OH, 1971.

An Important Word About References Pages

References pages give all writers nightmares. Finding the correct material for them can be tedious, and the only joy associated with their completion is that they usually represent the final stage of the writing. Further, you will find that many variations in the References page occur from journal to journal. Many journals prefer quotation marks around the titles of articles while others do not, and some journals do not require that the actual article title be cited on the References page. Given all these variations, your best bet is to choose a journal that is standard in your field (you can always ask a professor to recommend one) and consistently follow that citation style to the letter in your papers.

Also, you should be sure to label your References pages or Bibliography pages properly. Too many writers label a page "Bibliography" when they really mean "References," or vice versa, and this is especially confusing for professors if there is any discrepancy between the sources cited and those listed at the paper's end. To avoid problems, follow these guidelines:

- A *References* page contains only those references that were directly cited in the text.

- A *Bibliography* or *Selected Bibliography* page contains references referred to in the text plus the chief publications that you consulted in a general way.

- A *Notes* or *Endnotes* page refers to a page of *explanatory* as well as bibliographic information about those references cited in the text.

You may only be using References pages—not Bibliography pages or Endnotes pages—as an undergraduate, but as a graduate student or professional you may be attaching separate pages of explanatory notes or bibliographies. You are permitted to include *both* a References page and a Bibliography page at the end of a paper if you wish, but be certain that they are on separate pages and the distinction between them is clear.

Library Resources

> *Science is built up with facts, as a house is with stones. But a collection of facts is no more a science than a heap of stones is a house.*
> —*Jules Henri Poincaré*

So you have to use the library. You begin to feel as if you are trapped in a giant pinball game. You bounce around the walls and careen into various dead ends until something finally lights up. Or you suspect that you are really just an unwilling passenger stuck on the space shuttle on a purely scientific mission. Nevertheless, you have got to learn to use the library, especially any library that is specialized to your field. Library phobia is easily overcome with practice, and with the help of computers and the lists in this chapter you can find some of your most vital resources easily.

There are abundant gadgets in modern college and university libraries to help you find articles and books—some are even fun to use. In this chapter, I have listed some of the most commonly used books by field of study—which should save you some time—and I have chosen books that are standard enough to be in almost any academic library. Because nearly every academic library catalogs books according to the Library of Congress system, I have also identified the Library of Congress call numbers next to the book titles to make them easier to find. It is a good idea to browse through some of these books, particularly the dictionaries, just to become familiar with them. Researching a paper for a 300- or 400-level course may even require you to use abstracts or indexes, which are warehouses that list and describe articles that have been published in technical journals. As undergraduates, the most common general index you use to find technical articles is probably the *Applied Science and Technology Index*. You may not have to use indexes often, but simply ignoring them out of fear or laziness will cause you to miss some of your best resources, and if you go on to graduate school you will certainly have to become comfortable using them. At first indexes and abstracts can be confusing, but they always include sections on how to use them in the front or back, and often they are on CD-ROM as well.

Most commonly, you are just looking for introductory information, and therefore LIAS or a similar computer system that accesses library materials may be your quickest route. Also, technical dictionaries, encyclopedias, and other handbooks are especially nifty for finding definitions of specialized terms or for just getting background information. It is easy to forget that articles from the popular magazines (e.g., *Newsweek, Time, Garbage*) are often great resources too, especially when it comes to global or controversial issues, and you can easily track down such articles by using a computer system such as ProQuest, which is available in most libraries. ProQuest is sort of an expanded CD-ROM version of the *Reader's Guide to Periodical Literature* that you may have used in high school. With all of these things making the laborious thumbing-through of card catalogs almost obsolete, there is no excuse for not finding good research materials. Library staff are around to help you too—just ask.

There are all kinds of tricks smart students use when they research. At the end of an article or book, for instance, you will usually find a References section. It is practical, then, to track down related articles by using the References section itself as a resource instead of trying to start from scratch and wade through indexes. Professors and graduate students can give you tips on relevant articles too, and in many cases they will lead you to unpublished articles that you might not otherwise find. It is normal to have a hard time finding information at first, but you will find that key articles can pop up in an almost mystical fashion if you are tenacious. The bottom line is that you have to approach your library research just as you would any other research endeavor—with imagination, perseverance, and the good sense to ask for help when you need it.

Style Manuals

The Reference sections of libraries always have style manuals devoted to writing in the sciences and engineering, many of which have been published by professional organizations. These books are especially handy for checking a point of grammar while you are in the library, or for reading up on a conceptual level about a writing problem. What follows are some of the most current writing handbooks that libraries usually stock. I highly recommend *The McGraw-Hill Style Manual* and *The Elements of Style* as quick and easy-to-use reference tools.

STYLE MANUALS provide specific stylistic guidelines and answers to matters of grammar and format.

PN147.M47 1983	The McGraw-Hill Style Manual.
LB2369.D8 1962	A Manual of Form for Theses and Term Reports.
PE1475.S25 1994	Helping Researchers Write—So Managers Can Understand.
PE1408.S772 1959	The Elements of Style.
PE1478.D8	A Manual on Writing Research.
T11.M56	Writing for Technical and Professional Journals.
T11.K34 1985	Elements of the Scientific Paper.
T11.M418 1982	How to Write and Publish Engineering Papers and Reports.
PN187.C5	The "How to Write What" Book.
PE1408.F4773 1974	The Art of Readable Writing.
T11.M53	Technical Writing.
T11.E35	The Art of Technical Writing.
T11.D33 1988	How to Write and Publish a Scientific Paper.
T11.S65 1977	Technical Report Writing.
T11.M56 1968	Writing for Technical and Professional Journals.
PE1478.M8 1969	Engineered Report Writing.
QD85.A25 1986	The ACS Style Guide: A Manual for Authors and Editors.
PE1475.T53 1988	Effective Writing for Engineers, Managers, Scientists.

DICTIONARIES and HANDBOOKS define words and describe how to use them.

PE1693.G3 1990	Acronyms, Initialisms, & Abbreviations Dictionary.
PE1680.M59	Harper Dictionary of Contemporary Usage.
PE1591.M37 1962	Roget's International Thesaurus.
PE1680.R63 1957	The Word Finder.

General Resources for Science and Engineering

SCIENTIFIC DICTIONARIES provide specific meanings for words.

Q123.M15 1983	McGraw-Hill Dictionary of Scientific and Technical Terms.
QA5.J32 1976	Mathematics Dictionary.

ENCYCLOPEDIAS provide specialized background information.

Q121.M3 1982	McGraw-Hill Encyclopedia of Science and Technology.
QH540.4.M3 1980	McGraw-Hill Encyclopedia of Environmental Science.
AE5.E363 1990	Encyclopedia Britannica.

HANDBOOKS guide you to preliminary information.

TJ151.M371	Standard Handbook for Mechanical Engineers.
TK151.S8	Standard Handbook for Electrical Engineers.
QA47.M315 27th	CRC Standard Mathematical Tables.
QD65.H301	CRC Handbook of Chemistry and Physics.
T56 1971	Industrial Engineering Handbook.
TA151.S8	Standard Handbook for Civil Engineers.

ABSTRACTS AND INDEXES lead you to specific journal articles.

QD1.A51	Chemical Abstracts.
QA75.5.A25	ACM Guide to Computing Literature.
QA76.C5854	Computing Reviews.
G1.G36	Geo Abstracts.
TD180.P6	Pollution Abstracts.
HD9540.5.E55	Energy Index.
Z5322.E2E53	Environmental Index.
QA1.M76	Mathematical Reviews.
Z7401.S365	Science Citation Index.
QA276.A1 C87	Current Index to Statistics.
TN1.A58	Metallurgical Abstracts.

BUSINESS SOURCES describe industries, corporations, and products.

T12.T6Q	Thomas Register of American Manufacturers.
HC107.P4A282	Harris Pennsylvania Industrial Directory.
HG4057.A4	Standard & Poor's Register of Corporations, Directors and Executives.

CONFERENCE PROCEEDINGS lead you to papers given at conferences.

Z7401.I54	Index to Scientific and Technical Proceedings.
Z7409.D56	Directory of Published Proceedings.

BIOGRAPHICAL SOURCES give general information about scientists.

Q141.A47	American Men and Women of Science.
Q141.D5 1981	Dictionary of Scientific Biography.
T39.W5	Who's Who in Technology Today.

SCIENTIFIC DICTIONARIES provide specific meanings for words.

Q123.M15	McGraw-Hill Dictionary of Scientific and Technical Terms.
QE5.G37 1980	Glossary of Geology.
QC801.9.I5	International Dictionary of Geophysics.
QC854.G7 1972b	Meteorological Glossary.
TN10.C3	International Dictionary of Metallurgy-Mineralogy-Geology.

ENCYCLOPEDIAS provide specialized background information.

QH540.4.M3	McGraw-Hill Encyclopedia of Environmental Science.
QC852.A5	Compendium of Meteorology.
Check Call #	Encyclopedia of Earth Sciences Series.
TD351.T63	Water Encyclopedia.

HANDBOOKS guide you to preliminary information.

TD145.C2	CRC Handbook of Environmental Control.
QD951.W82	Crystal Structures.
QD65.H301	CRC Handbook of Chemistry and Physics.
QE515.W42	Handbook of Geochemistry.
GC24.C17	CRC Handbook of Marine Science.
QC861.B43	Handbook of Meteorology.

BUSINESS SOURCES describe industries, corporations, and products.

T12.T6 Q	Thomas Register of American Manufacturers.
HC107.P4A28	Industrial Directory of the Commonwealth of Pennsylvania.

ABSTRACTS AND INDEXES lead you to specific journal articles.

Z7913.I7	Applied Science and Technology Index.
Z6031.G4	Bibliography and Index of Geology.
QD1.A51	Chemical Abstracts.
QH541.C6	Computers in the Environmental Sciences.
Z5851.E62	Engineering Index.
G1.G36	Geo Abstracts.
QC851.A62	Meteorological and Geoastrophysical Abstracts.
QE351.M35	Mineralogical Abstracts.

TECHNICAL REPORTS give results of ongoing research.

QE1.U5	Open-file Reports. U.S. Geological Survey.

GUIDES TO THE LITERATURE list some of the best resources in the field.

Z7935.G45	Sources of Information in Water Resources.
T11.W741 1986	Writer's Guide to Periodicals in the Earth Sciences.
Z6031.W35	Geologic Reference Sources: A Subject Regional Bibliography of Publications and Maps in the Geological Sciences.

CURRENT AWARENESS SERVICES list the most recently published journal articles.

Z7141.C8701	Current Contents: Physical, Chemical, & Earth Sciences.

Earth Science Resources

Materials Science Resources

SCIENTIFIC DICTIONARIES provide specific meanings for words.

TN609.E4	Elsevier's Dictionary of Metallurgy.

ENCYCLOPEDIAS provide specialized background information.

TP9.E66	Encyclopedia of Chemical Processing and Design.
TP9.E685 1978	Encyclopedia of Chemical Technology.
TP156.P6E52	Encyclopedia of Polymer Science and Technology.

HANDBOOKS guide you to preliminary information.

TP151.C52 1973	Chemical Engineers' Handbook.
QD151.2.C64	Comprehensive Inorganic Chemistry.
QA483.H313 1958	Constitution of Binary Alloys.
QD951.W82	Crystal Structures.
TP815.E5	Engineering Properties of Selected Ceramic Materials.
TN690.P4	A Handbook of Lattice Spacings and Structures of Metals and Alloys.
TN690.v52	Pearson's Handbook of Crystallographic Data for Intermetallic Phases.
TN693. H4S313	Handbook of Refractory Compounds.
QD65.H301	CRC Handbook of Chemistry and Physics.
TA459.A5	Metals Handbook.
QD501.L592	Phase Diagrams for Ceramists.
TA459.A78 1983	ASM Metals Reference Book.
TN671.S55 1976	Metals Reference Book.
QE431.6.P5P73	1989 CRC Practical Handbook of Physical Properties of Rocks and Minerals.
TP360.H46 1978	Synthetic Fuels Data Handbook: U.S. Oil Shale, U.S. Coal, Oil Sands.

BUSINESS SOURCES describe industries, corporations, and products.

T12.T6 Q	Thomas Register of American Manufacturers.
TP809.5.C4	Ceramic Data Book Featuring Equipment and Materials.
TP1130.I5 1977	International Plastics Selector, 1977.

ABSTRACTS AND INDEXES lead you to specific journal articles.

Z7913.I7	Applied Science and Technology Index.
TP785.A64	Ceramic Abstracts.
QD1.A51	Chemical Abstracts.
Z7914.C4C85	Current Awareness in Particle Technology.
HD9540.5.E55	Energy Index.
Check Call #	Fuel and Energy Abstracts.
TN1.M53	Metals Abstracts.

TECHNICAL REPORTS give results of ongoing research.

Micro 4 OFR	Open-file Reports. U.S. Bureau of Mines.

GUIDES TO THE LITERATURE list some of the best resources in the field.

Z6678.S65 1965	Guide to Metallurgical Information.
Z7401.C48	Scientific and Technical Information Sources.

SCIENTIFIC DICTIONARIES provide specific meanings for words.

Q123.M15	McGraw-Hill Dictionary of Scientific and Technical Terms.
TN9.T5	Dictionary of Mining, Mineral, and Related Terms.
TN865.I43 1982	The Illustrated Petroleum Reference Dictionary.
TN10.C3	International Dictionary of Metallurgy-Mineralogy-Geology.

ENCYCLOPEDIAS provide specialized background information.

TP9.E685	Encyclopedia of Chemical Technology.
TP9.E66	Encyclopedia of Chemical Processing and Design.

HANDBOOKS guide you to preliminary information.

TP151.C52 1973	Chemical Engineers' Handbook.
TD145.C2	CRC Handbook of Environmental Control.
TN870.Z2 1970	Practical Petroleum Engineers Handbook.
TN151.S18	SME Mining Engineering Handbook.
TN23.U42	Mineral Facts and Problems.

BUSINESS SOURCES describe industries, corporations, and products.

T12.T6 Q	Thomas Register of American Manufacturers.
Z7164.P94W33	Commodity Prices, a Source Book and Index.
TN257.M5	Mineral Exploration, Mining, and Processing Patents.
TS670.A47	Metal Finishing Guidebook-Directory.
TN800.B57	Coal Information Sources and Data Bases.
HD9540.3.W67	World Coal Industry Report and Directory.

ABSTRACTS AND INDEXES lead you to specific journal articles.

Z7913.I7	Applied Science and Technology Index.
HD9540.5.E55	Energy Index.
Z5851.E62	Engineering Index.
TA706.R53	Geomechanics Abstracts.
HD9506.A2M445	Mineral Economics Abstracts.
TN860.P398	Petroleum Abstracts.

TECHNICAL REPORTS give results of ongoing research.

Micro 4 OFR	Open-file Reports. U.S. Bureau of Mines.

GUIDES TO THE LITERATURE list some of the best resources in the field.

Z7401.C48	Scientific and Technical Information Sources.

Mineral Economics and Mineral Engineering Resources

Life Science Resources

SCIENTIFIC DICTIONARIES provide specific meanings for words.

Q123.M34 1989	McGraw-Hill Dictionary of Scientific and Technical Terms.
QH302.5.M3	McGraw-Hill Dictionary of the Life Sciences.
R121.S8	Stedman's Medical Dictionary.
S411.D57	A Dictionary of Agriculture and Applied Terminology.

ENCYCLOPEDIAS provide specialized background information.

Q121.M3 1987	McGraw-Hill Encyclopedia of Science & Technology.
QL3.G7813	Grzimek's Animal Life Encyclopedia.
SB317.58.E94	The New York Botanical Garden Illustrated Encyclopedia of Horticulture.
TX349.F58	Foods and Food Production Encyclopedia.

HANDBOOKS guide you to preliminary information.

QH310.A392 1972	Biology Data Book.
QL55.M45	CRC Handbook of Laboratory Animal Science.
RS51.M4 1989	Merck Index.
TD194.6.E5	Environmental Impact Data Book.

BUSINESS SOURCES describe industries, corporations, and products.

R712.A1A6 1986	American Medical Dictionary.
R118.4.U6M4 1988	Medical and Health Information Directory.
TS803.H3	Directory of the Forest Products Industry.
TP248.3.I5601	The Biotechnology Directory.

ABSTRACTS AND INDEXES lead you to specific journal articles.

Check call #	Abridged Index Medicus.
Check call #	Biological Abstracts.
Z7401.I54	Index to Scientific and Technical Proceedings.
Z7401.S365	Science Citation Index.

TECHNICAL REPORTS give results of ongoing research.

Z1223.A18	Monthly Catalog of United States Government Publications.
Z7913.U2	Government Reports Announcement and Index.

GUIDES TO THE LITERATURE list some of the best resources in the field.

Z7401.M28	Science and Engineering Literature.
Z5071.G83	Guide to Sources for Agricultural and Biological Research.

CURRENT AWARENESS SERVICES list the most recently published journal articles.

Check call #	Current Contents: Agriculture, Biology, and Environmental Sciences.
Check call #	Current Contents: Life Sciences.

Chemistry and Chemical Engineering Resources

SCIENTIFIC DICTIONARIES provide specific meanings for words.

Q123.M34 1989	McGraw-Hill Dictionary of Scientific and Technical Terms.
QD5.B4 1986	Concise Chemical and Technical Dictionary.
TP9.G28 1978a	Handbook of Chemical Synonyms and Trade Names.

ENCYCLOPEDIAS provide specialized background information.

Q121.M3 1987	McGraw-Hill Encyclopedia of Science and Technology.
TP9.E685 1978	Encyclopedia of Chemical Technology.

HANDBOOKS guide you to preliminary information.

QC61.A5 1972	American Institute of Physics Handbook.
QD65.H301	CRC Handbook of Chemistry and Physics.
TP151.P45 1984	Perry's Chemical Engineers' Handbook.
T55.3.H3S3 1989	Dangerous Properties of Industrial Materials.
QD51.S88 1990	CRC Handbook of Laboratory Safety.

BUSINESS SOURCES describe industries, corporations, and products.

T12.T601 Q	Thomas Register of American Manufacturers.
TP200.C4 Q	Chemical Profiles.
HD9651.3.C43	OPD Chemical Buyers Directory.
Z7164.P94W33	Commodity Prices: a Source Book and Index.

ABSTRACTS AND INDEXES lead you to specific journal articles.

Z7913.I7	Applied Science and Technology Index.
QD1.A51	Chemical Abstracts.
Check call #	Chemical Titles.
Z7401.I54	Index to Scientific and Technical Proceedings.

TECHNICAL REPORTS give results of ongoing research.

Z1223.A18	Monthly Catalog of United States Government Publications.
Z7913.U2	Government Reports Announcement and Index.

GUIDES TO THE LITERATURE list some of the best resources in the field.

QD8.5.B6 1979	Use of Chemical Literature.
QD8.5.M34	How to Find Chemical Information.
QD8.5.M44 1982	Chemical Publications, Their Nature and Use.
QD8.5.W54 1991	Chemical Information Sources.

CURRENT AWARENESS SERVICES list the most recently published journal articles.

Z7141.C8701	Current Contents: Physical, Chemical, & Earth Sciences.

Mathematical Science Resources

SCIENTIFIC DICTIONARIES provide specific meanings for words.

QA5.J32 1976	Mathematics Dictionary.
QA276.14.K46 1982	A Dictionary of Statistical Terms.
QA76.15.R67 1987	Dictionary of Computers, Information Processing, and Telecommunications.
QA76.15.D526 1990	Dictionary of Computing.

ENCYCLOPEDIAS provide specialized background information.

QA5.I8313 1987	Encyclopedic Dictionary of Mathematics.
QA40.V18 1989	The VNR Concise Encyclopedia of Mathematics.
QA276.14.E5	Encyclopedia of Statistical Sciences.
QA76.15.E48	Encyclopedia of Computer Science and Engineering.
QA76.15.E5	Encyclopedia of Computer Science and Technology.

HANDBOOKS guide you to preliminary information.

QA47.H3201	CRC Handbook of Mathematical Sciences.
QA331.S685 1987	An Atlas of Functions.
QA40.H34 1983	Handbook of Applied Mathematics, Selected Results, and Methods.
QA276.25.B48 1968	CRC Handbook of Tables for Probability and Statistics.
QA76.5.H3544 1984	The Handbook of Computers and Computing.
QA76.M37 1983	The McGraw-Hill Computer Handbook.

BUSINESS SOURCES describe industries, corporations, and products.

HD9696.C63U51521	Data Sources. Vol. 1. Hardware.
HD9696.C63U515301	Data Sources. Vol. 2. Software.
HD9696.C63U51522	Data Sources. Vol. 3. Data Communications/Telecommunications.

ABSTRACTS AND INDEXES lead you to specific journal articles.

QA1.M76	Mathematical Reviews.
QA276.A1C87	Current Index to Statistics, Applications, Methods, and Theory.
HA1.S72	Statistical Theory and Method Abstracts.
QA75.5.A25	ACM Guide to Computing Literature.
QA76.C5854	Computing Reviews.
QA76.I4601	Computer and Information Systems Abstracts Journal.
Z6654.C17Q3501	Computer Literature Index.
Q334.A77	Artificial Intelligence Abstracts.

TECHNICAL REPORTS give results of ongoing research.

Q334.5.S34 1988	The Artificial Intelligence Compendium, Abstracts and Index to Research on AI Theory and Applications.

GUIDES TO THE LITERATURE list some of the best resources in the field.

QA41.7.U83	Use of Mathematical Literature.
QA41.7.S3	Using the Mathematical Literature, a Practical Guide.
Z7551.B86	How to Find Out About Statistics.
QA76.C6501	Computing Information Directory.

SCIENTIFIC DICTIONARIES provide specific meanings for words.

QC5.D55	Dictionary of Physics and Mathematics Abbreviations, Signs, and Symbols.
QB14.H69 1980	Glossary of Astronomy and Astrophysics.
QB14.F3 1985	The Facts on File Dictionary of Astronomy.
Q123.M34 1989	McGraw-Hill Dictionary of Scientific and Technical Terms.
QC5.T5 1979	Concise Dictionary of Physics and Related Subjects.

ENCYCLOPEDIAS provide specialized background information.

Q121.M3 1987	McGraw-Hill Encyclopedia of Science and Technology.
QB43.2.C35	The Cambridge Encyclopedia of Astronomy.
QC5.E52	Encyclopedic Dictionary of Physics.
QC5.E545 1991	The Encyclopedia of Physics.

HANDBOOKS guide you to preliminary information.

QC61.A5 1972	American Institute of Physics Handbook.
QB63.B898 1978	Burnham's Celestial Handbook; an Observer's Guide to the Universe Beyond the Solar System.
QD65.H301	CRC Handbook of Chemistry and Physics.
QB461.L36 1980	Astrophysical Formulae: a Compendium for the Physicist and Astrophysicist.
QB64.R58 1979	Astronomy Data Book.
QB64.R5913 1975	Astronomy: a Handbook.

BUSINESS SOURCES describe industries, corporations, and products.

Z7551.S84	Statistics Sources; a Subject Guide to Data on Industrial, Business, Social, Educational, Financial, and Other Topics for the United States and Internationally.

ABSTRACTS AND INDEXES lead you to specific journal articles.

Z7913.I7	Applied Science and Technology Index.
Z5153.A862	Astronomy and Astrophysics Abstracts.
QD1.A51	Chemical Abstracts.
Q1.S3	Physics Abstracts.
Check call #	Chemical Titles.
Z7401.S365	Science Citation Index.

TECHNICAL REPORTS give results of ongoing research.

Z7913.U2	Government Reports Announcement and Index.
Z1223.A18	Monthly Catalog of U.S. Government Publications.

GUIDES TO THE LITERATURE list some of the best resources in the field.

Z5151.S38 1982	A Bibliography of Astronomy.
Z5151.S4	A Guide to the Literature of Astronomy.
QC5.45.U73	Use of Physics Literature.

CURRENT AWARENESS SERVICES list the most recently published journal articles.

Z7141.C8701	Current Contents: Physical, Chemical, & Earth Sciences.

Physics and Astronomy Resources

Aerospace, Mechanical, Electrical, And Nuclear Engineering Resources

SCIENTIFIC DICTIONARIES provide specific meanings for words.

Q123.M34 1989	McGraw-Hill Dictionary of Scientific and Technical Terms.
TK7885.A2S56	Microcomputer Dictionary.
TK9.I478 1977	IEEE Standard Dictionary of Electrical and Electronics Terms.
TL509.G86 1986	Jane's Aerospace Dictionary.
Q123.D37 1976	French-English Science and Technology Dictionary.

ENCYCLOPEDIAS provide specialized background information.

Q121.M3 1987	McGraw-Hill Encyclopedia of Science and Technology.
TA402.E53 1986	Encyclopedia of Materials Science and Engineering.

HANDBOOKS guide you to preliminary information.

TJ151.M395 1986	Mechanical Engineer's Handbook.
TK151.M64 1985	Electrical Engineer's Reference Book.
TJ263.H38 1983	Heat Exchanger Design Handbook.
TK7871.85.H336	Handbook on Semiconductors. vol. 1-4.
TA418.9.C6H33	Handbook of Composites.
TA459.A5	Metals Handbook.

BUSINESS SOURCES describe industries, corporations, and products.

T12.T6 Q	Thomas Register of American Manufacturers and Thomas Register Catalog File.
HC107.P4A282	Harris Pennsylvania Industrial Directory.
TL512.W6	World Aviation Directory.

ABSTRACTS AND INDEXES lead you to specific journal articles.

Z7913.I7	Applied Science and Technology Index.
Z5851.E62	Engineering Index.
TA1.A63953	Applied Mechanics Reviews.
Q1.S3 Sect. B	Electrical and Electronics Abstracts (Section B of Science Abstracts).
HD9540.5.U501	Energy Research Abstracts.
TL500.I57	International Aerospace Abstracts.
Z7401.S365	Science Citation Index.

TECHNICAL REPORTS give results of ongoing research.

Z7913.U2	Government Reports Announcement and Index.
Z1223.A18	Monthly Catalog of United States Government Publications.
TL500.S35	STAR: Scientific and Technical Aerospace Reports.

GUIDES TO THE LITERATURE list some of the best resources in the field.

T10.7.I54 1985	Information Sources in Engineering.
T10.7.M68 1976	Guide to Basic Information Sources in Engineering.
T10.7.S93	Scientific and Technical Information Resources.

CURRENT AWARENESS SERVICES list the most recently published journal articles.

T1.C78	Current Contents: Engineering, Technology, & Applied Sciences.

SCIENTIFIC DICTIONARIES provide specific meanings for words.

Q123.M34 1989	McGraw-Hill Dictionary of Scientific and Technical Terms.
TD173.T83	Dictionary of Dangerous Pollutants, Ecology, and Environment.
TA9.S35 1980	Dictionary Of Civil Engineering.
S411.D57	A Dictionary of Agriculture and Allied Terminology.
Q123.D37 1976	French-English Science and Technology Dictionary.

ENCYCLOPEDIAS provide specialized background information.

Q121.M3 1987	McGraw-Hill Encyclopedia of Science and Technology.
NA31.E59 1988	Encyclopedia of Architecture, Design, Engineering, & Construction.

HANDBOOKS guide you to preliminary information.

T56.23.H36	Handbook of Industrial Engineering.
TA151.S8 1983	Standard Handbook for Civil Engineers.
TA658.3.B85 1987	Building Structural Design Handbook.
TH151.T55 1982	Time-Saver Standards for Architectural Design Data.
TD145.C2	CRC Handbook of Environmental Control. vol. 1-5.

BUSINESS SOURCES describe industries, corporations, and products.

T12.T6 Q	Thomas Register of American Manufacturers and Thomas Register Catalog File.
HC107.P4A282	Harris Pennsylvania Industrial Directory.
TA215.S85	Sweets Catalog File: Products for Industrial Construction and Renovation.

ABSTRACTS AND INDEXES lead you to specific journal articles.

Z7913.I7	Applied Science and Technology Index.
Z5851.E62	Engineering Index.
Z5941.A66	Architectural Index.
TD180.P6	Pollution Abstracts.
Z5074.E6A4	Agricultural Engineering Index.
7401.S365	Science Citation Index.

TECHNICAL REPORTS give results of ongoing research.

Z7913.U2	Government Reports Announcement and Index.
Z1223.A18	Monthly Catalog of United States Government Publications.

GUIDES TO THE LITERATURE list some of the best resources in the field.

T10.7.I54 1985	Information Sources in Engineering.
T10.7.M68 1976	Guide to Basic Information Systems in Engineering.
T10.7.S93	Scientific and Technical Information Resources.

CURRENT AWARENESS SERVICES list the most recently published journal articles.

T1.C78	Current Contents: Engineering, Technology, and Applied Sciences.

Environmental, Architectural, Agricultural, Industrial, And Civil Engineering Resources

Resumes, Letters, and Graduate School Application Essays

Chapter 8

*A thought that sometimes makes me hazy, am I,
or are the others crazy?*
                    —*Albert Einstein*

Usually, seeking a job or applying to grad school is at least a 400-level course in itself, and this chapter is a great place to begin studying. You can not allow a poorly thought-out resume, letter, or application essay to sink you, and no one expects you to invent these documents from thin air. Remember, you are often competing with hundreds of similar documents at a time, so you want yours to fit in yet stand out for the right reasons. This usually means that you must revise and revise and revise and customize your resume and letters to increase your odds. Further, you must treat your resume as a living, changing document that you will revise for the rest of your life. Most professionals change jobs five or more times, so their resumes are always in flux. You will find that the best way to write good resumes, professional letters, and grad school application essays is to base them on good models—know the conventions and know just how far you can stretch them. There are lots of models in this chapter that will help you to do just that.

When it comes to interviews, all sorts of scenarios are possible. When I was an undergraduate hunting for a job, an interviewer once began a discussion with me by saying simply "Tell me about yourself." After ten minutes of nervous talking I paused, and the interviewer leaned back further in his chair, laced his fingers over his stomach, and said. "Tell me more about yourself." A friend of mine conducts interviews for a Pennsylvania environmental agency, and she actually keeps track of all the "likes," "and stuffs," and "you knows" she hears during the interview, each one increasing the odds against the interviewee. Some interviewers are very aggressive, and some seem to be even more nervous than you are. You can not anticipate what will happen in your case, but you can prepare yourself by reviewing the tips presented in this chapter.

Finally, seek help. Other readers—your peers, your professors, and the assistants at your university or college Career Development

Center—can add fresh and healthy perspectives (and even corrections) to your resumes, letters, and essays for graduate school applications. Do not settle for less than collective agreement that you have presented yourself in the best possible way. It pays off.

Writing Resumes

Here is one place where you should simply follow the accepted models as closely as you can, adding minor variations sparingly and only to augment individuality. You must make your resume as accessible and immediately scannable as possible, so stick to the proven conventions (i.e., do not do things such as switch the "Education" and "Experience" sections—you will only confuse your readers). Think of your audience's needs rather than your own, and use your common sense—the honor of winning first place at a local bar's Joke-Off Contest in January is obviously not worth including on your resume, for instance. The bottom line is that your resume is a SUMMARY of your skills and an ARGUMENT that you are worth hiring; select and condense your material accordingly. Also, keep a copy of the resume and cover letter that you use to apply for a position; you should review them if you have to prepare for a follow-up interview. The best way to begin writing a resume is to mimic the qualities of a good model, so, with the help of your peers, I have provided you with excellent resume models on the following pages, and the general advice below will also help you to get kicked off properly.

Overall Mechanical Guidelines

- If possible, limit your undergraduate resume to one page.

- Typed text is essential, and laser printout is preferred.

- Keep at least one-inch margins on all four sides of the page, and spread your information out so that it is visually balanced and highly readable.

- Use varying margins to enhance the overall scannability, but keep identical margins for related information (i.e., line up your major sections with each other; line up your job descriptions with each other, etc.).

- Overall, your guideposts are SPACE and SPECIFICITY: only include information that is worth the space it takes up, and always use specifics to outline your qualifications.

- Exploit punctuation marks—especially dashes, semicolons, and colons—to present your material efficiently, but be sure that you are using and typing the marks correctly.

- Be line conscious: if you are fighting for space and you see that just one or two words are gobbling up an entire line unnecessarily, revise things accordingly; two "Relevant

Courses Completed" can usually fit on one line, for example.

- Present the final version of your resume on durable white or off-white paper; avoid odd colors such as purple or green.

- Do not use too many fancy fonts or too many capital letters, and when you do use different fonts and point sizes use them with consistency and common sense (i.e., if you boldface one job title, boldface them all).

- Proofread with precision, even having someone else proof-read the resume too—grammatical errors are the number one reason that many resumes are passed by.

- As you look over your completed resume, consider VISUAL BALANCE and EASY SCANNABILITY. Revise accordingly.

Name and Addresses

- There is no title for this section; simply provide your legal name, addresses, and phone numbers as shown in the examples.

- Boldfacing and capitalizing your name is reasonably standard, though not required, and making your name stand out with a larger or fancier font is acceptable, but beware of overkill.

- Do not use titles such as "Resume" or "Personal Data Sheet" on the top of the page; your name centered at the top automatically tells readers that the document is a resume.

Objective

- As a rule of thumb, always include a job objective on an undergraduate resume. Keep it as short as is practical, with the goal of taking up no more than two lines of text.

- If possible, use an actual job title ("forecaster," "materials specialist") and provide the specific type of employer or type of position that you are seeking ("a mining company," "a research facility," "a consulting firm").

- Avoid phrases such as "a challenging position," "a progressive company," "an established firm"—you do not want to sound like you are preaching to them about what they should be. Your aim here is to categorize the role that you can fulfill.

- Your job objective can be tailored a bit to the position that you are applying for, but never mention a company's actual name in your job objective—the objective is intended to define a role, not a specific job at a specific place.

Education

If you hold more than one degree, list them in reverse chronological order—most recent first. Write out the correct title of your school and write out your exact degree, including a minor if it is to your advantage. Include your projected graduation date even if it is years away. Options that might be included under "Education":

- *G.P.A.* Generally, include it if it is near a 3.0 or better, and include G.P.A. in major if it is impressive.

- *Dean's List.* Provide actual semesters or years.

- *Relevant Course work.* List actual course titles or appropriately worded categories.

- *Curriculum Description.* Could be included to describe your background concretely.

- *Study Abroad.* Always include it and provide the college's name.

- *Honor's Program.* Always include it.

- *Thesis.* Always include it and list it by title.

Note the variety of approaches and options explored under "Education" in the sample resumes provided.

Experience / Work Experience / Employment

- Any of these titles is acceptable, though "Experience" is the most standard.

- Use past tense throughout this section, even to describe jobs that you currently hold.

- As a rule, list your work experience in reverse chronological order—most recent first—and provide the actual dates of employment. Provide exact job titles (invent them honestly if no actual titles were used), and give the locations of your employers. All jobs need not be directly relevant to the position you are applying for, but be sure that the descriptions of your job duties are worded such that they enhance your accomplishments and responsibilities.

- Use active verbs to describe your job skills (a handy list is provided just after this section of the manual) and make each job description specific and efficient, but do not always feel compelled to describe your duties ("waiter" and "newspaper carrier," for example, are self-explanatory).

- As a rule, do not include your supervisor's name or phone number here, unless you are applying for an internship (where formal applications are rare).

- Including job salaries is rarely a good idea, but providing the number of hours you worked per week can be impressive.

- Overall, use identical margins for parallel items (e.g., line up all of your job titles with each other) and be certain that your material is easy to scan. Again, the sample resumes provided show a variety of approaches.

Activities / Honors / Professional Activities

- For this section, choose whichever title or combination of titles best fits your actual examples. "Activities" is the most commonly used.

- Dates are optional, but they can be used to illustrate your level of participation in activities.

- List the most noteworthy extracurricular activities and include offices that you have held. Include any honors you have received, especially scholarships, but do not repeat items that were included in other sections of the resume.

- Choose descriptions of your leisure activities wisely and sparingly, even to the point of presenting them all on one line for the sake of efficiency.

- The bottom line in this section is that you want to enhance your uniqueness, whatever that uniqueness is: a volunteer firefighter, eagle scout, or licensed pilot can stand out as much as a scholarship recipient or professional sorority officer.

References

This section is optional because employers already know that you can provide them with references. If you do include this section keep it highly efficient, and be sure to ask your references for their permission first if you include their actual names as references. As a rule, however, do not include the actual names of your references on your resume unless you are simply seeking an internship; for a full-time permanent position you want your resume to inspire the employer to contact you and specifically request your references. Employers are often looking for specific kinds of references, and you do not want to hurt your chances by listing references who might not be quite right for their needs, or giving an employer the opportunity to call or write one of your references without your knowing about it.

Creating Your Own Category

In addition to the above standard categories, you may add a special category to your resume and locate it wherever it seems most logical. Such a category should enhance your individuality as it applies to the position that you are seeking. "Computer Skills," "Military Service," or "Other Professional Training" are examples of typical special categories. Just be sure that you have something substantial and relevant to say, and, as always, be space-conscious and efficiency-minded.

The Graduate Student Resume

Full instruction about graduate student resumes is beyond the scope of this manual, but here are a few tips:

- Graduate student resumes adhere to the same basic principles as undergraduate resumes, but they tend to be longer than one page. The material on each page should be equally balanced if possible, so that no page contains just a few lines, and so that each page works as independently as possible.

- You may include additional categories such as "Professional Qualifications," "Teaching Experience," "Presentations," and "Publications." Categories such as "Teaching Experience" and "Publications" are especially important for any graduate student applying to an academic post.

- Those things listed under "Publications" need not actually be published, but should have been submitted to a journal or presented at a professional conference.

Action Words That Help You To Describe Your Skills In The "Experience" Section Of Your Resume And In Cover Letters.

Accepted	Achieved	Adapted	Adjusted
Administered	Advised	Allocated	Analyzed
Appraised	Approved	Arranged	Assembled
Assessed	Assigned	Assisted	
Balanced	Budgeted	Built	
Calculated	Catalogued	Checked	Clarified
Classified	Collected	Communicated	Compared
Compiled	Composed	Computed	Conceived
Conducted	Confronted	Constructed	Consulted
Contracted	Controlled	Converted	Conveyed
Coordinated	Correlated	Counseled	Created
Critiqued			
Decorated	Defined	Delegated	Demonstrated
Designed	Detailed	Determined	Developed
Devised	Diagnosed	Digitized	Directed
Discovered	Displayed	Dissected	Distributed
Drafted			
Earned	Edited	Effected	Empowered
Encouraged	Enforced	Engineered	Enlarged
Enlightened	Enlisted	Established	Estimated
Evaluated	Examined	Executed	Expanded
Experienced	Experimented	Explained	
Facilitated	Financed	Formed	Formulated
Founded			
Generated	Governed	Grouped	Guided
Handled	Headed	Helped	
Implemented	Improved	Improvised	Increased
Indexed	Informed	Initiated	Innovated
Inspected	Inspired	Installed	Integrated
Interpolated	Interviewed	Investigated	
Justified			
Keynoted			
Led			
Made	Maintained	Managed	Mapped
Measured	Mediated	Modeled	Moderated
Monitored	Motivated		
Navigated	Negotiated	Nominated	
Observed	Operated	Ordered	Organized
Originated	Overcame		

Participated	Performed	Persuaded	Pioneered
Planned	Predicted	Prepared	Presented
Presided	Prioritized	Produced	Programmed
Promoted	Protected	Provided	

Questioned

Recognized	Recommended	Reconciled	Recorded
Recruited	Reorganized	Reported	Researched
Retrieved	Reviewed	Revised	

Scheduled	Screened	Served	Shaped
Simplified	Solved	Sorted	Sparked
Strengthened	Supervised	Systematized	

Trained	Transcribed	Transformed	Translated

Unified	Utilized

Validated	Verified

Wrote

MATTHEW A. SILICA

Home:
1886 Fork Road
York, PA 17407
(717) 238-4486

School:
3007-C Vairo Blvd.
State College, PA 16803
(814) 764-2259

Objective   To enhance professional breadth through a summer internship position in materials science and engineering.

Education   **Bachelor of Science in Ceramic Science and Engineering**
The Pennsylvania State University, University Park, PA 16802
Anticipated Graduation, May 1992. Current GPA: 3.05/4.0.

Bachelor of Arts in Natural Sciences, Co-op Engineering Program
Lock Haven University, Lock Haven PA 17745

Work Experience   White Rose Roofing, Inc. York, PA.
1988, 1989, 1990, during summer and winter breaks.
As part of a team, I installed new roofing systems and repaired old and damaged roofs.
SUPERVISOR: John Cutter, (717) 645-6693.

Stevenson Library, Lock Haven University, Lock Haven, PA.
1988, 1989, during academic year.
I worked in the Reader Services Office 10-15 hours per week, documenting newly arrived materials and answering questions from library patrons.
SUPERVISOR: Bruce E. Bookish, (717) 399-4487.

Weathershield, Inc., York, PA.
1986, 1987, during summer and winter breaks.
I assisted in the insulation of over 20 new and existing homes, working 50+ hours per week.
SUPERVISOR: Wilma Fiber, (717) 462-0065.

Activities   Sigma Pi Fraternity—treasurer and chair of membership committee.
Member of Management Science Club and the Ski Club.
Volunteer for the Red Cross.

Language/ Computer Skills   Six years of written and oral Spanish.
Working knowledge of Pascal, BASIC, and introductory CAD systems.
Working knowledge of word processing using Microsoft Word and Macwrite.

References

Dr. Gary Messing
119 Steidle Building
University Park, PA 16802
(814) 865-2262

Mr. Bruce Bookish
Lock Haven University
Lock Haven, PA 17745
(717) 399-4487

Mr. John Cutter
237 Rosemont Avenue
York, PA 17408
(717) 645-6693

Sample Resume

JANICE MOBILE

Current Address
136 Eden Lane
Pleasant Gap, PA 16802
(814) 236-6778

Permanent Address
1306 North Dallas Parkway
Dallas TX 75420
(214) 609-9612

OBJECTIVE   Position with a mining company in production or engineering.

EDUCATION   The Pennsylvania State University, University Park, PA
Bachelor of Science in Mining Engineering, May, 1992.

Relevant
Courses:

Mine Maintenance Engineering	Mine Systems Engineering
Mining Engineering Analysis	Elements of Mineral Processing
Senior Mining Engineering Project	Rock Mechanics
Mineral Processing Laboratory	Mine Plant Engineering
Mineral Land and Mine Surveying	Mineral Property Evaluation

EXPERIENCE   **Engineering Assistant**, Cyprus,Inc., Waynesburg, PA

5/89-8/89
4/88-1/89

-Participated in an Engineering Student Co-op program and gained diverse experience in the operation of a longwall mine.
-Assigned to Engineering Department but also worked for other departments, including production, safety, and maintenance.
-Performed surveying, data compilation, and time-study tasks.
-Completed computer simulations for ventilation and belt haulage.
-Participated in quantity and pressure ventilation surveys.

5/87-8/87

Roofbolter Helper, Solar Fuel Company, Grindstone, PA
-Began as a surface and underground laborer for a room and pillar mine.
-Was promoted to a steady roofbolter helper position on a single-boom machine for final two months; also performed other working face duties.

5/86-8/86

Laborer, Deerfield Coal Company, Irwin, PA
-Performed minor land improvements on reclaimed properties.

5/85-8-85

Laborer, FCI Corporation, Irwin, PA
-Operated a forklift and made deliveries of machined parts.

1/84-8/85

Stockperson, World of Values, Dallas, TX

COMPUTER SKILLS   Experienced with IBM's Lotus 1-2-3, Penn State's Mine Ventilation Simulation program, and West Virginia University's Belt Haulage Simulation program.

ACTIVITIES   Student member of the Society of Mining Engineers, 1988-1990.
Active in racquetball, water-skiing, and canoeing.

REFERENCES   Letters of reference provided upon request.

Dennis Marble

Present Address
1297 East Hamilton Avenue
State College, PA 16801-5331
(814) 861-3767 *

Permanent Address
123 Macintosh Drive
Coraopolis, PA 15108-2757
(412) 230-9208

OBJECTIVE   Seeking an analyst position with a consulting firm where I can apply and enhance my mineral economics and business logistics training.

EDUCATION   The Pennsylvania State University, University Park, PA
Bachelor of Science in Mineral Economics, Minor in Business Logistics
Graduation date: May 1992

WORK EXPERIENCE

- Salesman, The Oxford Shop, State College, PA. June 90-present.
  Responsible for cash register, inventory control, customer service, and ordering merchandise in a men's clothing store.
  Developed radio and newspaper advertising campaign.
  Programmed computer for inventory, mail order, and sales projection.

- Research Assistant, Penn State Department of Economics. Summer 90.
  Assisted an Economics professor with library research, computer programming, word processing, and filing.
  Programmed computer code to evaluate data for the self-employed in the United States.
  Utilized various computer packages including SAS, Word Perfect, and Lotus 1-2-3.

- Owner, Manager. Foley Lawn Service, Coraopolis, PA. Summer 89.
  Started own business for lawn service and general handyman work.
  Employed three high school students, organized payroll, developed business contracts with residential and civic groups, maintained equipment, and developed advertising.

ACTIVITIES

- The 1991 Penn State Dance Marathon. Rules and Regulations Chairperson
  Helped organize the largest student-run philanthropy in the country.
  Supervised 50 students in the areas of registration and security.
  Redesigned rulebook and registration processes.
  Supervised registration.

- Theta Chi International Fraternity
  Held the offices of Vice President, Social Chairman, and Caterer.
  Developed chapter philanthropy that benefited terminally ill children.

HONORS

- Theta Chi Penn State Chapter Outstanding Brother of the Year, 1989-1990.

- Theta Chi International Fraternity Active Chapter Service Award, 1989.

- Theta Chi International Fraternity Key Man Award, 1987, 1989.

- IBEW/NCEA Scholarship Recipient, 1986

Sample Resume

JANE SAMPLE

<u>Current Address</u>
999 Lions Hall
University Park, PA 16802
(814) 861-2233

<u>Permanent Address</u>
111 East Street
Johnstown, PA 15905
(814) 235-2656

OBJECTIVE   To obtain an entry-level position in the testing, analysis, or manufacture of ceramic substrates or integrated circuits.

EDUCATION   The Pennsylvania State University, Park, PA
<u>B.S. in Ceramic Science and Engineering,</u>
Anticipated Graduation—May, 1991
Thorough engineering curriculum in the processing and electrical, optical, mechanical, and thermal properties of ceramics and glass, with electives in circuit analysis and semiconductor physics.

G.P.A.: 3.45/4.0
THESIS: Rapid Thermal Sintering of Nanocrystalline Ceramic Films.

EXPERIENCE   <u>IBM</u>, Burlington, VT., SUMMER PRE-PROFESSIONAL (5/90-8/90).
-Developed quantitative and qualitative procedures for analyzing solder using x-ray fluorescence.
-Analyzed solder samples to assure that the solder met impurity specifications.
-Studied the effects of grain boundary diffusion in metals.
-Evaluated the accuracy and reliability of the x-ray fluorescence results against other analytical tests.

<u>Penn State Dept. of Engineering Mechanics</u>, TYPIST (1/90-5/90).
-Used a word processor to type course notes for a graduate engineering mechanics seminar.

<u>Penn State Office of Disabilities</u>, PROCTOR (1/89-1/90).
-Proctored handicapped students during examinations and provided physical assistance as needed.

<u>Johnstown Civic Band</u>, Johnstown, PA., MUSICIAN (6/87-12/89).

HONORS/   Dean's List (1989-1990).
ACTIVITIES   Member of the American Ceramic Society (1988-1990).
President of Keramos - National Honor Society for Ceramic Engineers (1989-1990).
Recipient of the Ferro Corporation Scholarship (1990).
Member of Earth and Mineral Sciences Student Council (1989-1990).
Recipient of the Cook Memorial Scholarship (1989).
Academic Chairperson for Residence Hall (1987).

Julie Pedate

1104 East Foster Avenue, #2124
State College, PA 16803
(817) 987-5004

OBJECTIVE

A position involving research and development of improved or novel bio-materials or bioceramics for use in orthopedic applications.

EDUCATION

<u>Masters of Science</u>, Ceramic Science
January 1994-present
The Pennsylvania State University, University Park, PA 16802

THESIS: "Infiltration of Continuous Fiber-Reinforced Composites."

<u>Bachelor of Science</u>, Ceramic Science and Engineering
August 1989-May 1993
The Pennsylvania State University, University Park, PA 16802

THESIS: "Sol-Gel Derived Alumina."

PROFESSIONAL EXPERIENCE

The Pennsylvania State University January 1994-present
<u>Graduate Assistant</u> — University Park, PA
Responsible for conducting research on thesis project, teaching undergraduate labs, and grading exams. Current thesis research involves investigating a novel approach to the fabrication of composites via nitrate melt infiltration of multi-fiber towns.

The Pennsylvania State University May 1993-December 1993
<u>Researcher</u> — University Park, PA
Investigated particulates in membranes associated with aseptic loosening of hip prosthesis. Characterized collagen, gelatin, and hydroxyapatite with Raman spectroscopy, electrophoresis, electronic measurements, and SEM.

The Pennsylvania State University August 1992-May 1993
<u>Director of Earth and Mineral Sciences Computer Center</u> — University Park, PA Renovated existing facilities, which included the acquisition and installation of new computers and software. Organized and taught classes in introductory Microsoft Word, Cricket Graph, and Excel.

PROFESSIONAL EXPERIENCE (continued)

Howmet Corporation   June 1992-August 1992
Summer Engineering Intern — Whitehall, MI
Investigated quality control and mechanical property effects of excess sodium on Al_2O_3-based investment casting molds with various testing methods, including physical testing (hot/cold MOR, compression, XRD) and chemical analysis.

Alcoa Technical Center   July 1991-August 1991
Summer Engineering Intern — Alcoa Center, PA
Performed electrical resistivity and optical measurements on Al_2O_3 substrates.

The Pennsylvania State University   January 1990-May 1991
Research Assistant — University Park, PA
Prepared sol-gel samples, tested samples using tensile and compressive techniques, assembled and tested strain gage rosettes.

PAPERS

"The System Al_2O_3-N_2O_5-H_2O at Various Temperatures," presented at the annual meeting of the Materials Research Society, Minneapolis, 1995.

"The System MgO-P_2O_5-H_2O at 25°C," submitted to the *Journal of the American Ceramic Society.*

ACTIVITIES

Member of the Society for Biomaterials (1993-present).
Member of Keramos (1995-present).
Recipient of the Ellen Steidle Award for Outstanding Service, College of Earth and Mineral Sciences, Penn State. (1993)
Member of the American Ceramic Society, Penn State Student Chapter (1989-present).
Member of the Society of Women Engineers (1989-1993); Executive Board Member (1991-1992).
Guides for the College of Earth and Mineral Sciences (1990-1993); Chair (1991-1993).
Earth and Mineral Sciences Student Council (1990-1993); Secretary (1991-1992).

As with resumes, great professional letters tend to be based on excellent models, so the next few pages provide models that you can use. The best tip that I have heard on letter writing is that the letter is for the audience, not for you. Sure you are selling yourself, but you do that by molding your skills to what an employer needs and by knowing all that you can about your audience. This tells you that you should do such things as read the company literature and have a specific person's name and title to write to (you can always request this by phone before you write). The same is true for graduate school letters, which should be tailored specifically to the program where you are applying. In sum, know what your audience is interested in and how you might fit into their plans, not the other way around.

Types of letters that you may need to write include:

- A *Standard Cover Letter,* usually introducing your resume and requesting an interview.

- A *Thank You Letter,* expressing thanks for an interview or invited visit.

- An *Acknowledgment Letter,* acknowledging the receipt of a job offer or some materials.

- A *Query Letter,* making a specific request for information.

- A *Letter of Decline or Acceptance,* declining or accepting a job offer.

- A *Graduate School Essay,* seeking admission into a particular program.

Overall Mechanical Guidelines

- Limit letters to one page if at all possible, and type them using single-spaced or 1.5-spaced typing.

- Skip lines between paragraphs.

- Keep at least one inch margins on all four sides of the page, and spread your information out so that it is visually balanced.

- Use short paragraphs rather than long ones.

- Avoid contractions.

- No fancy fonts and nothing visually unusual here—be highly conventional.

- Proofread carefully and present the final version of the letter on durable white or off-white paper.

The Heading and Greeting

- At the top right hand of the page, put the date, your address, and your phone number. Below that, at the left margin, put the name, title, and address of the person receiving the letter.

- Skip a space or two, then write "Dear," the person's title (Dr., Ms., Mr.), name, and a colon.

- You should always find out the proper title, spelling, and gender of the receiver of the letter (all it takes is a phone call), but if you can not be certain whether the receiver of the letter is male or female, it is acceptable to use both the first and last name (i.e., "Dear Jan Morris").

The Opening Paragraph

- If appropriate and possible, open with a reference to how you derived knowledge of the company or position.

- Include any relevant dates or names here to provide context for the letter (e.g., "I was pleased to speak with you over the phone on March 3 about the opening for..."). Otherwise, simply be forthright about why you are writing the letter ("I am writing to you because...").

- Include details about the company's specific activities if possible—show them you have done your homework.

- Introduce yourself concretely. Your opening paragraph shows the employer what you know about them and introduces you to them briefly; or, if they have previously heard from you, the opening paragraph provides a new context for the letter that you are writing.

The Middle Paragraph(s)

- One paragraph may suffice here, but use more if necessary.

- Stick to one topic per paragraph.

- If this is a cover letter, introduce your resume ("As the enclosed resume shows...") and *interpret* it for your audience rather than simply repeat its details. Apply your education, work experience, and activities directly to the job, proving that you are unique and extremely capable.

- If this is a letter other than a cover letter, use the middle paragraph(s) to concretely and briefly review your credentials as they apply to the position you are after.

- Do not be too cocky, aggressive, idealistic, or unrealistic; come off as mature, self-aware, and confident.

The Closing Paragraph and Graceful Exit

- Keep your closing short and simple. Do not waste time. Respectfully indicate your desire for further action if appropriate, reminding the company of your availability.

- Remembering that a company could try to call you over a break or during the summer, indicate those phone numbers that are relevant right in the text.

- Be gracious and sincere, not falsely flattering or too pushy.

- Under the final paragraph, skip a space or two, then, directly under your heading address, type "Sincerely," or some other appropriate closing, then handwrite and type your name underneath.

- If an enclosure (such as a resume) is included along with the letter, note this with the word "Enclosure" at the left margin near the bottom of the page.

Because you must be so space-conscious and line-conscious in your resumes and letters, using the state two-letter abbreviations below is a good way to tighten up your text. Note how both letters in each abbreviation are capitalized with no periods following them.

State Two-Letter Abbreviations

Alabama	AL	Alaska	AK	Arizona	AZ
Arkansas	AR	California	CA	Colorado	CO
Connecticut	CT	Delaware	DE	District of Columbia	DC
Florida	FL	Georgia	GA	Hawaii	HI
Idaho	ID	Illinois	IL	Indiana	IN
Iowa	IA	Kansas	KS	Kentucky	KY
Louisiana	LA	Maine	ME	Maryland	MD
Massachusetts	MA	Michigan	MI	Minnesota	MN
Mississippi	MS	Missouri	MO	Montana	MT
Nebraska	NB	Nevada	NV	New Hampshire	NH
New Jersey	NJ	New Mexico	NM	New York	NY
North Carolina	NC	North Dakota	ND	Ohio	OH
Oklahoma	OK	Oregon	OR	Pennsylvania	PA
Rhode Island	RI	South Carolina	SC	South Dakota	SD
Tennessee	TN	Texas	TX	Utah	UT
Vermont	VT	Virginia	VI	Washington	WA
West Virginia	WV	Wisconsin	WI	Wyoming	WY

January 23, 1992

999 Lions Hall
University Park, PA 16802
(814) 861-2233

Dr. Timothy Brown, Manager
General Technology Division
International Business Machines Corporation
Burlington, VT 19000

Dear Dr. Brown:

After working for IBM and speaking with you about ceramic substrates in electronic packages over the summer, I have become interested in permanent employment in your Burlington branch. As you know, I am currently a senior Ceramic Science and Engineering student at Penn State, and I am seeking an entry-level position that involves working with the materials utilized in electronic packages.

Experiencing IBM first-hand was gratifying and exciting. Not only was I impressed with the concern IBM has for the safety of its employees, but I was intrigued by its constant striving to become a six-sigma company. Along with this goal, IBM faces the challenge of producing electronic packages that operate faster and are not limited by the speed of the substrates. I want to be a part of a team that faces and meets these kinds of challenges.

As my enclosed resume shows, I have gained valuable experience from both school and employment. My academic background includes studies of various properties of ceramics with an emphasis in electrical properties of materials and integrated circuits. I have also expanded my studies by taking electives in the computer graphics area. Through my employment as a summer pre-professional for Quality Assurance under Dr. George Slusser, I was exposed to several analytical techniques to assure the purity of materials used in chip production. In particular, I was faced with the task of developing procedures to analyze materials using x-ray fluorescence. As a result, I was able to validate my findings by comparing them to the findings obtained from accurate though more tedious analytical techniques. I am confident that my background, particularly my previous employment at your Quality Assurance division, will be of interest to you.

After you have reviewed my qualifications, I would welcome the opportunity for an interview. I can be reached at 814-861-2233. I look forward to hearing from you soon.

Sincerely yours,

Jane Sample

Enclosure

March 4, 1992

614 Mountainside Avenue
State College, PA 16801
(814) 869-6623

Mr. Jack Sinclair
Amoco Production Company
P.O. Box 1234
Denver, CO 80202

Dear Mr. Sinclair:

The January issue of *Oil and Gas Journal* indicates that Amoco
Production Company is actively exploring in the area of the
Overthrust Belt. I am interested in training and working as a geophysi-
cist in this area for your company.

My preparation in Penn State's earth sciences program has equipped
me with a strong background in both the theory and practical applications of geophysics. As part of my Bachelor of Science degree, I have
taken two special courses in seismic methods, a course in well log
analysis, and have completed a senior thesis on seismic interpretation.
I also have had a summer field experience as a geophysicist trainee,
working with both data processing and special stratigraphic interpretive projects. The company that employed me last summer—Rockell
Company, Boulder, Colorado—even chose my report on my summer
field experience as a model for this summer's interns. I am confident
that I can enrich my skills as a geophysicist with Amoco.

My resume is enclosed for your reference. I am readily available to
meet with you and discuss career opportunities with Amoco
Production Company, and I would welcome a personal interview. If
you need further information, I can be reached at (814) 869-6623, or,
on the chance that you are unable to contact me, my parents can be
reached at (717) 643-9056. I look forward to hearing from you soon.

Sincerely,

Jason Terranes

Enclosure

Sample "Blind" Cover Letter

February 8, 1991

444 Montrose Avenue
State College, PA 16801
(814) 235-6783

Ms. Gale DeLaveaux
E304/C216
DuPont Experimental Station
Wilmington, DE 19880-0304

Dear Ms. DeLaveaux:

At the suggestion of Dr. John Hellman, Assistant Professor of Ceramic Science and Engineering at the Pennsylvania State University, I am writing to inquire about any possible summer internship positions for 1991. I understand that you are working with thermodynamic, kinetic, and finite element modeling of reactions and flow in CVD reactors.

I am currently a junior in Ceramic Science and Engineering at Penn State. As my enclosed resume shows, I have a thorough background in mathematics, chemistry, and physics, and I am enthusiastic about applying this background in a summer position where I will learn from experienced scientists in a research environment. My primary interests are in thermodynamics and processing, and my interests continue to expand as my education broadens.

I am eager to discuss my background with you at your convenience. Dr. Karl Spear (814-865-4992), chair of the Ceramic Science and Engineering Program at Penn State, is also happy to speak with you about my credentials. My daytime phone number is (814) 235-6783, and a secondary phone number, where you could leave a message, is (814) 236-5609.

Thank you for your consideration.

Sincerely,

William Scaffold

Enclosure

April 8, 1995
927 W. Barnard St. Apt.#1
State College, PA 16801
(827) 841-6836

Wilson Geosciences
379 Sonoma Lane
Sonoma, CA 95476

Dear Personnel Representative:

I will be graduating in May from Penn State University with a degree in Geosciences (emphasizing hydrogeology and geochemistry) and am seeking employment as an entry-level hydrogeologist.

There are three primary skills that I have developed to apply as an entry-level hydrogeologist:

1. Field skills and experience, which are usually primary responsibilities in entry-level positions. I have conducted my own research for my senior thesis, which involved implementing borehole dilution tests to determine the groundwater velocity in a coal aquifer. I also have extensive course-work field experience, ranging from summer field school to water and soil sampling at polluted sites.
2. A strong interest in contaminant transport and groundwater modeling. This interest, coupled with good computer skills, provides opportunities for the use of groundwater and chemical modeling software packages. Hydrogeology and geochemistry course work have equipped me with the theoretical basis for modeling, and an introduction to software packages. My work experience has involved extensive PC skills. Although I have had only preliminary opportunities to apply these skills to groundwater modeling packages, I am confident that I can become proficient with these packages.
3. Good communication skills. Good writing and speaking skills allow for effective communication within a company and with clients. My studies have provided me with quality writing experience. I am currently completing my senior thesis, which involves both written and oral presentation. Throughout my studies, I actively worked to improve my writing and gain experience writing for a variety of audiences.

My resume is enclosed for your reference. I would welcome the opportunity to meet with you to discuss my career opportunities with your company. Please feel free to contact me at (827) 841-6836. I look forward to hearing from you.

Sincerely,

Diane Z. Weston

Enclosure

May 13, 1991

789 Allenway Building
310 South Allen Street
State College, PA 16801
(814) 230-1443

Dr. William Fielding, Materials Specialist
Allegheny General Hospital
320 East North Avenue
Professional Building, Suite 201
Pittsburgh, PA 15212

Dear Dr. Fielding:

Thank you for taking the time to speak with me on Monday, May 2. It was obvious from all the activity that you had a demanding schedule that day, and I appreciate your fitting me in so readily. During our walking tour, I was especially impressed with the plans for the new biomedical laboratory; Allegheny General Hospital is obviously a progressive facility.

As I trust our discussion made clear, my primary interest is biomaterials and I share your belief that a materials scientist is a necessary addition to your team. Over the past year I have come to realize that the impact of materials in orthopedic applications is just beginning to be investigated in depth, and the prospect of working in a biomedical lab where such materials are developed is particularly exciting.

I look forward to hearing from you about Allegheny General Hospital's hiring plans soon, and I thank you again for all your personal and gracious attention.

Cordially,

Julie Pedate

February 12, 1991

1298 Geary Hall
University Park, PA 16802
(814) 239-4656

Dr. Janis Jingle
Sharp Metal Company
642 Southeast King's Road
Port Orchard, WA 98366

Dear Dr. Jingle:

I was pleased to receive your kind letter of February 5, 1991, offering me a position as a metallurgist with Sharp Metal Company. My visit in December confirmed for me that it is an honor to be considered for employment with Sharp Metal.

At this time, personal considerations make it impossible for me to respond to your offer immediately. I do understand, however, that you need my decision by April 1, 1991, and I will notify you as soon as possible before that date. I appreciate your patience.

You will be hearing from me soon.

Sincerely yours,

Robert Annealer

Sample Letter Accepting A Job Offer

April 22, 1992

544 Heritage Oaks
Oak Lane
State College, PA 16803
(814) 861-2390

Ms. Alice Jenkins, Personnel Manager
Coalburn Company, Inc.
534 Manor Circle
Denver, CO 80909

Dear Ms. Jenkins:

It is a pleasure to acknowledge your letter of April 13 offering me a position as a Mining Engineer with Coalburn Company at a yearly salary of $32,000. I am delighted to accept this offer, and I warmly thank you for the confidence in me that your job offer reflects.

I understand that the conditions of employment require me to pass a physical examination and complete my bachelor's degree here at Penn State in May.

As you suggested, June 1, 1991, is a convenient starting date for me, and I am happy to accept your offer of two weeks of temporary housing while I locate an apartment. As always, Coalburn Company has been highly hospitable and friendly in its dealings with me, and I look forward to a challenging and rewarding career with you.

Please contact me if you need any further information.

Sincerely,

Joshua Carboni

A standard part of a graduate school application calls for you to write an essay as part of your petition for admission. This essay is highly important, and it is given as much or even more weight than the reputation of your undergraduate degree program, your grades, etc. Typically, you are asked to summarize your academic and even your personal background, discuss any summer work, research, or teaching you have been involved in, and define your short-term and long-term goals. The following advice and the sample essays will help you to prepare a professional essay.

Answer Each Part Of The Essay Question Explicitly

Count the parts of the essay question, even the implied parts. Be certain to address each one, perhaps devoting a separate paragraph to each. If you like, you can use the same terminology of the essay question (e.g., "long-term goals," "research endeavors"), especially in your topic sentences, to form individual paragraphs. Provide transitions among the parts as well.

Choose A Narrative, Research, Or A Teaching Approach

Since your essay is a document unto itself, it should work as an individual piece. You might choose a narrative approach to discuss your background and your motivation for further study, or a research or teaching approach to underscore what you will be doing in graduate school. With a narrative approach, of course, beware of being overly chatty and nonprofessional, and with a research or teaching approach beware of sounding too clinical.

Discuss Your Background Concretely And Professionally

As with a resume, the essay is your best and sometimes only chance to summarize your accomplishments in summer work, research, course work, and activities. The essay can directly influence the decision of whether you are a good person to hire as a graduate assistant. Therefore, in your essay paragraphs, provide the same kind of concrete detail you would include on a resume, emphasizing hands-on work and accomplishments: hardware and software you have worked with; internships you have completed; professors you have worked with; theses you have written; offices you have held, etc.

Learn All You Can About The Program You Are Applying To

Learning all you can about the program not only makes sense, it gives you concrete material to include in your essay. One phone call to the graduate office of the program will secure you plenty of materials and information about the faculty, and some students even go so far as to read some of the faculty publications to familiarize themselves with the research being done. You may even be expected to discuss a particular faculty member whom you would like to work with or the type of project you would like to work on, and such details can heavily affect your chances of acceptance. Use your resources—current professors, graduate students, the library, the graduate program itself—to increase your odds and improve your essay.

<u>Graduate School Application Essay for the University of Washington</u>

Shelby Lapp

Currently, I am involved in research under the supervision of Dr. Michael Arthur. Together we are investigating the accumulation and preservation of organic material in Peru Margin sediments. I am specifically interested in the role of oxygen and other controls on organic preservation. My research includes analysis of organic and inorganic carbon concentration in the sediments using a carbon coulometer, and the use of RockEval pyrolysis and mass spectrometry to determine the source and maturity of the organic material. I hope to continue to investigate this and other related subjects in my graduate research.

Given my interests in oceanography, geoscience, and climate change, I would like to focus my graduate studies in the area of carbon and nutrient cycling in the oceans and the role of these cycles in global change. I will particularly emphasize resuspension and remineralization at the sediment-water interface. Ultimately, my graduate program will reflect my diverse interests, but it will also connect these broad areas into a coherent project which I can support with my course work. In pursuing a graduate degree, I hope to strengthen my research abilities and to broaden my knowledge in oceanography and geochemistry.

In undertaking graduate study, I am highly interested in attending an institution at which there are strong programs in both chemical and geological oceanography, because my research interests are firmly rooted in both areas. In this respect, the University of Washington's diverse faculty and state-of-the-art research facilities are ideal for my needs.

My long-term professional goal is to pursue a research position in which I can investigate both theoretical and environmental components of geochemical oceanography. I have spoken with a number of my current professors about the relative merits of continuing my work in academia and feel that eventually I would be well-suited for a faculty position. I hope that the admissions committee will find my background and my goals to be compatible with graduate study at the University of Washington.

Sample Graduate School Application Essay — Research Approach

*Sample
Graduate
School
Application
Essay —
Narrative
Approach*

Personal Essay
by Richard Long

My first personal introduction to the profusion of environmental laws in our country came while working for my father. I worked for over eleven years at my father's business, Long's Exxon Service Center. While there, I performed every job, task, and duty associated with the operation of a service station. One duty involved the maintenance of records for the underground storage tank field on the site. I was amazed at the amount of paperwork required to comply with the laws governing underground tanks.

My two years of full-time work after high school taught me much about myself, but I realized that I needed a different environment to continue growing. Therefore, from 1986 to 1990, I attended classes at Montgomery County Community College while continuing to work at Long's Exxon. I was certain I would eventually choose a science-related major, but an event in 1991 showed me that geology was what I wanted to pursue. In 1991, during the installation of a new, larger underground field tank at the station, an environmental consulting firm tested our soil and found hydrocarbon levels just above the allowable limits. Seventy tons of soil had to be removed from the site and incinerated at great expense to my father's business. These environmental regulation problems that my father had as a small business owner made me realize that eventually I wanted to make it easier on other small business owners to comply with environmental laws.

I transferred to the Pennsylvania State University as an undergraduate in geosciences in 1992, where I tailored my courses to environmental geology and hydrogeology. My senior thesis directly reflects my career goals. I am working with the United States Department of Agriculture on a study of riparian zones and their favorable effects on elevated nitrate levels in ground water due to farm fertilization practices. Meanwhile, I am developing a shallow subsurface geologic map of a riparian zone using seismic refraction techniques. This map will allow a first-order approximation of ground-water flow at the field site and also guide the installation of hydrogeologic equipment by the USDA. I now understand more fully how geophysical methods serve an important role in environmental work, and my senior thesis is a good introduction to this field.

I had initially intended to acquire a position with an environmental consulting firm upon graduation, but discussions with several of my professors indicated that I would be much better prepared for the job market if I earned a Master of Science in Geological Sciences. Therefore, I wish to continue my education in order to strengthen my background in geophysical methods in environmental geology. I am especially interested in refraction and resistivity techniques. Pursuing my master's degree in eastern Pennsylvania will also expose me to the geographical region and environment I will someday work in as a professional.

Think Through the Application Process First

Before you approach any potential recommender, identify the number of letters that you will need and the type of materials that you have to prepare. Doing so helps you figure out what each recommender's role should be and how to discuss the application with him or her.

Use Application Materials to Help You Choose Recommenders

If they are applicable, application materials are your best ally in choosing the right recommenders. Some application materials, for instance, encourage you to choose professors who can truly speak to your teaching ability or character rather than those with the highest stature. Take this advice seriously.

Seek a Mix of Recommenders, and Identify Their Roles for Them

Your recommenders collectively should reflect a balanced picture of you. A Truman Scholarship winner from a few years ago chose the following recommenders: a University program coordinator, an assistant professor of political science, and a Red Cross coordinator. If your recommender is expected to comment from a certain type of angle, be sure he or she knows this.

Choose Recommenders Who Know You Well and Help Them to Know You Better

Avoid abruptly asking a professor for a recommendation letter after class or in the hallway. Instead, make an appointment to discuss whatever you are applying for and what his or her role can be. If possible, give the professor any materials that might help him or her write a more detailed letter, such as your resume or an essay you have written, especially if the essay is related to course work you completed with the professor.

Respect a "No"

If someone you ask for a letter seems to be saying "no" to you, seek someone else. The person may be inappropriate, too busy, or may not know you well enough to write you a good letter.

Allow the Letter to be Confidential and Let the Recommender Discuss Your Grades

On an application form, you will usually be asked if you wish to waive (give up) your right to see your recommender's letter. Do so. The recommender will then be more comfortable and probably more genuine too. Also, the policy at many schools is that a professor can not technically reveal your grades or G.P.A. unless you give written permission. Those who review your application know your grades anyway, and the professor will probably want to discuss them for your benefit, either to applaud them or to help explain any inconsistencies, so provide your professor with a signed note granting him or her permission to discuss your grades.

Provide the Recommender with a Firm Deadline and a Stamped Addressed Envelope

This just takes some simple preparation. Be sure that you know who the letter is to be addressed to, and, as a professional courtesy, give the recommender a stamped addressed envelope to mail it in. Provide an exact deadline for the letter's completion and gently remind the recommender of it later if necessary.

Begin to Recognize Yourself as a Professional

When you apply for a job, graduate school, or a scholarship, you are confidently stepping up a rung on a long academic or professional ladder. Act accordingly by taking yourself and your recommenders seriously. Do not undermine what you are applying for or be self-deprecating. Articulate some goals for yourself. Write them down if it helps. Respect and consider any coaching or coaxing the recommender offers. Help the recommender get to know you as a student and as a person.

Interviews can be scary, and it is easy to respond to them by being either overnervous or overcocky. It is important, then, to prepare for an interview as you prepare for any test. The bottom line is to prepare well, and one of the best ways to do this is simple and fundamental: REVIEW YOUR RESUME AND COVER LETTER BEFORE YOUR INTERVIEW. An interviewer will probably have your resume or cover letter right there on the desk as a reference tool, so you should be prepared to answer questions based on those materials. Have a verbal resume in mind when you go in. Here is a quick synopsis of interview tips:

Tips For Interviews

What To Do:

- Review your resume and cover letter to prepare for the interview.
- Read company literature and review any personal correspondence from the company.
- Be prompt, neat, and courteous.
- Listen attentively and speak intelligently—do not rush it.
- Be prepared to ask relevant questions.
- Try to sense when you have fully answered a question or when the interviewer is waiting to ask one.
- Express enthusiasm, but be realistic about your expectations of the job.

What Not To Do:

- Criticize yourself.
- Freeze or become tense, emotional, or impatient.
- Interrupt the interviewer's questions or speak out of turn.
- Oversell your case, try to be too funny, or act cocky.
- Make uninvited or elaborate promises.
- Draw out the interview or try to over control it.
- Linger over fringe benefits or starting salary.
- Speak too colloquially ("You know, it's like, I don't know, I'm like, clueless, you know?")
- Speak too formally, overusing passive voice or avoiding the use of "I."

Qualities That You Should Enhance in an Interview:

- Communication skills.
- Motivation and willingness to accept responsibility.
- Self-confidence, decisiveness, stability, and maturity.
- Perseverance, energy, common sense, and tact.
- Amiability and loyalty.

The Top Reasons Why Job Seekers Are Rejected:

- Lack of enthusiasm and interest; no evidence of initiative; no concrete goals; lack of maturity.
- Poor personal appearance; extreme or careless dress.
- Poor scholastic record or few extra-curricular activities without reasonable explanation.
- Excessive interest in salary, benefits, or promotion.
- Lack of interest in or knowledge of the company.
- Poor presentation of self; therefore, lack of poise, poor personality or abrasive manner, lack of confidence, timid or hesitant approach, arrogant or conceited attitude, poor speech habits.

Journal Articles About Writing

Chapter 9

This is the type of arrant pedantry up with which I shall not put.
—Winston Churchill, commenting on the notion that a sentence may not end with a preposition.

Here we take a look into the horse's mouth, or sit in the editor's or professor's armchair, as it were. If it is not obvious to you yet it will be soon: not only English teachers care if your writing is stylish and correct—your professors care, employers care, and the editors of magazines and journals certainly care. This chapter offers proof. There is plenty of stylistic advice available out there in the scientific journals themselves, indicating that editors and journal readers do indeed expect scientists and engineers to write clearly. In this chapter I have harnessed just a sampling of the good advice that is out there waiting for you.

Here is a quick summary of the chapter's contents:

"Comments From Some Miffed Editors" and the "Comments" sequel are specific tips from some irritated but nevertheless well-meaning and buoyant journal editors about what kinds of errors cross their desks in all-too-generous handfuls. Anyone in the earth sciences or related fields will certainly benefit from reading these articles and keeping them on hand, and others will find them illuminating as well.

"The Science of Scientific Writing" is my summary of a thoroughly detailed and important article about scientific writing from the journal *American Scientist.* You will find generalized and practical advice on how literally to put sentences together; your reading of this summary will make your writing task easier and help you to help your readers. Graduate students and professors are especially appreciative of this article.

"Advice to Scientist Writers: Beware Old 'Fallacies'" underscores how, as writing practices change, we must change with them—and at times we even must challenge advice about writing that we have heard all our lives. "Always use passive voice," "Never end a sentence with a preposition," "Never open a sentence with a conjunction": these are just some of the tidbits of advice that the author attacks. And she is funny too.

"The Universal Recipe For Scientific Reports" is a detailed look at how the best writers put together and publish their scientific reports in journals. The beauty of this piece is its universality and comprehensiveness; by definition, the advice in this article crosses disciplinary lines and serves as a first-rate guide for anyone intending to publish an article in a journal.

Finally, for professors and students who use this manual, I offer you "A Bibliography of Additional Journal Articles About Writing." This bibliography gives you one way to begin to find articles within your field that are similar to those in this chapter—my final spike to drive home the point that editors, scientists, and engineers want to read good writing. Do not just take my word for it; listen to the veterans in your field.

Comments From Some Miffed Editors

The comments that follow appeared in a recent issue of the *Geological Society of America Bulletin* (1) and they are reprinted here in their entirety with the authors' permission, copyright © 1989 by the Geological Society of America, Inc. These comments illustrate just how important it is that, as a scientist-writer, you choose your words with great care and with their literal meaning in mind. To emphasize their points, the editors even occasionally resort to sarcasm!

An increasing number of GSA members lament the general deterioration in the quality and clarity of writing by earth scientists. They complain especially about the misuse and overuse of words and phrases that lead to vague, awkward, or cumbersome sentences, and that require several readings before a meaning is derived. It may be only coincidental that the derived meaning is the one intended by the author.

Insofar as it is one of the duties or prerogatives of editors to educate potential or eventual authors, when necessary or appropriate, we offer this commentary as some of our "suggestions to authors." Our suggestions should not be regarded as "GSA style"; however, authors may find some red or purple ink in manuscripts that cross our desks if those authors misuse or overuse the words and phrases discussed below.

- We may say "volcanics," "clastics," "metamorphics," "metasediments," "intrusives," and "granitics" to each other in the field, but it is quite improper grammatically to add an "s" to an adjective to make a plural noun. It may be tedious and repetitious to read, but it is correct and unambiguous to write "volcanic rocks," "clastic rocks," "metasedimentary rocks," "intrusive rocks," and "granitic rocks."

- The terms "lithologies" and "mineralogies" should never be used until and unless we accept "geologies," "biologies," and "zoologies." Replace them with "rocks" or "rock types," and "minerals." "The lithology of a study area" and "the mineralogy of a suite of rocks" are quite correct phraseology.

- Many writers of geologic literature use "compression" indiscriminately for both stress and strain, as in the context of "compressional structures." Geologic structures are manifestations of strain; thus, in rock mechanics the convention is that "tension" and "compression" are terms that should be used in discussions of stress; whereas the corresponding strain terms are "extension" or "elongation," and "contraction" or "shortening" or even "constriction."

- It has come to seem that a paper is not "scientific" unless it contains two words: "essentially" and "constrain," preferably together in the construction "essentially constrains." Both are perfectly good, although overused, words, and they have their place in good writing. The English language is rich in other words, however, that may be used effectively to convey more explicit meaning, including "generally," "commonly," "typically," "nearly," "almost," "mainly," "chiefly," "partly," "characteristically," "usually," and "largely." Writers may find that "control," "limit," "restrict," "bound," "define," "contain," "characterize," and "restrain," and their related nouns are more meaningful than "constrain" and its related noun "constraint."

- The sentence "evidence suggests that the Earth is flat" carries no information. *What kind* of evidence? Geologic? Geodetic? Compelling? Permissive? Pseudo-scientific? Circumstantial? Specious? Just as vague for the same reason is the statement "data suggest that the Earth is flat." Imaginary data?

- At the same time, "data," "strata," "phenomena," and "spectra" are *plural.*

- We prefer to avoid using "evidence" as a verb, as for example, in the sentence "the presence of snakes in the grass was evidenced by their rattling sounds." We also maintain that the verb "postulate" is more euphonious than "hypothesize."

- Strictly speaking, the whole "comprises" its parts, but our dictionaries *(Webster's II New Riverside Dictionary, The American Heritage Dictionary)* say that the jury is almost evenly divided on its formal use, and that "comprise" may be used as a synonym for "consists of," "is composed of," "encompasses," and so on, but "comprised of" is wrong.

- Our dictionaries also say that "occur" and "occurrence" are better used when "happen" and "happening," respectively, can be substituted. Rather than "the rocks occur in the cliff," it is better to say "the rocks are in the cliff," "the rocks are present in the cliff," or "the rocks are exposed in the cliff." We expect that paleontologists will complain, however, because the "occurrence of fossils" is deeply rooted in the literature.

- The word "portion" is preferred when the word "share" can be substituted for it. Otherwise use "part," which is no less a profound or erudite word.

- "Suggest" is a frequently overused "weasel word" in manuscripts. Many writers build a house of cards with "suggest," when stronger words such as "indicate," "imply," "show," and "prove" may be more appropriate. Authors commonly write "Joe Schmoh *suggested* that the Earth is flat," when in fact Schmoh may have "proposed," "concluded," "indicated," "maintained," "asserted," "inferred," "implied," "stated," "believed," "postulated," "thought," "guessed," or "considered" that the Earth is flat. Other "weasel words" and phrases include "probably," "appears to be," "seems to be," "may be," and "could be." Their overuse should be avoided as much as possible.

- "Show" is being overused, however. "The outcrop shows iron stains" is better expressed, in our opinion, by "the outcrop *is* iron stained" or "the outcrop *has* iron stains."

- The awkward use of the infinitive "to be" is surfacing in scientific writing with increasing frequency, such as in "Joe Schmoh thought the Earth to be flat," or "Joe Schmoh showed the rock to be lithified." It is more straightforward to write "Joe Schmoh thought that the Earth was flat" and "showed that the rocks are lithified." Here is another example of vagueness: "Statistics reveal April's GNP to be lower than March's." Does that sentence mean that the April GNP *is* lower than March's or that it *will* be lower?

- "Since" is a *time* word; so also are "occasional," "while," and "frequently." "Occasional outcrops of obsidian were observed since the bulldozer passed through the hill." Were the outcrops there only on Tuesdays *because* the bulldozer passed through, or only on Tuesdays *after* the bulldozer passed through? Use "whereas" in place of "while" in those cases where time is not implied.

- We have yet to read an article that stated the *velocity* of a "rapid facies change." We have observed and mapped *abrupt* facies changes, however.

- "Sediments" are rock-disintegration products, such as sand, silt, and gravel. We would like to be invited to go on a field trip to see "Ordovician sediments." Although we realize that sediments were deposited in basins of Ordovician age, we'll bet 30¢ that they are "sedimentary rocks" today and should be so called.

- Because *lines* "trend" and "plunge," and *surfaces* "strike" and "dip," it is incorrect to say "northwest-trending faults," whereas "northwest-striking faults" is correct. Authors may object that the traces of faults on maps are lines, but because a map almost always represents the horizontal plane, the intersection of a fault surface with the map surface is a unique line: the strike.

- It is also increasingly common to see authors put together a string of nouns to construct what they believe is a more educated or profound name for a very simple thing, such as a "single component rock sample acquisition system" (five nouns to mean *rock hammer).*

- We believe that it is preferable to write "margin of the plateau," instead of "the plateau's margin," because inanimate objects cannot possess.

- Can anyone tell us what "packages" or "packets" are in the geologic context, and where either is formally defined? We can cite several different sizes and shapes of things that "package" has been used to describe, including an individual stratum, several strata, a sequence of stratified rocks, a temporal sequence of rocks, an areally restricted outcrop of a distinctive rock or group of rocks, fault blocks—even tectonic terranes. The definition that makes the most sense to us is that "package" and "packet" are the latest geologic buzzwords. So is "scenario," which ought to be replaced with "hypothesis."

The *Chicago Manual of Style* is a standard for scientific journals and is probably the best reference for these matters. We have learned that a new edition of *Suggestions to Authors of Reports of the U.S. Geological Survey*, a long-time standard for authors, may be printed soon. Melba Murray has just published a second edition of her excellent book, *Engineered Report Writing*. We also recommend Robert L. Bates' new little book, *Writing in Earth Science*, published by AGI ($3.95); it covers 95% of the "housekeeping" problems we encounter.

A nd now the sequel to the previous article, from the July 1990 issue of *Geological Society of America Bulletin* (2), copyright © 1990 by the Geological Society of America, Inc. The following comments are reprinted with the generous permission of the authors, who show that they are even capable of spirited jokes amidst their pleas for improved style.

Even More Comments From The Same Miffed Editors

The positive reaction of many Bulletin readers to our September 1989 Comments about misuse and overuse of words emboldens us to write a sequel. First, we wish to share the readers' views on some of our comments about style.

To our assertions that it is poor style to allow inanimate objects to be possessive, Robert Bates snorted: "Does that mean I should not say 'the rocket's red glare,' or 'the dawn's early light?' Nuts!" We respond, "touché!" He also said that his university has a department of classics, and although he realized that it probably should be properly termed Department of Classical History and Literature, he wasn't going to tell that department to change its name. We agree with him on that point, but we still think it is poor style to make plural nouns out of certain geologic adjectives, such as "lithic" to "lithics," and "clastic" to "clastics." Similarly, making "basaltic" into "basaltics," and "geologic" into "geologics" should also be discouraged.

Dr. Bates shared some other pet peeves with us, including "little pomposities" such as "prior to" for "before" and "is dependent upon" for "depends on." He said, "Encountered in reading, these are like the bump-bump, bump-bump on an old highway. They don't slow you down much, but they take a lot of pleasure out of the trip."

Several readers maintained that language actively evolves, and that we editors should flow with that tide, because rigorous editing may stultify creativity. We appreciate these sentiments, and we encourage innovation, but we maintain that poor syntax, excessive jargon, or prolific buzzwords may obfuscate an author's message. It is the author's scientific responsibility to write a story that readers will understand, rather than to make an exercise in creative prose. The editor's responsibility is to help an author present his/her message as clearly and succinctly as possible for the majority of readers. As an example, we shall continue to ask authors to rewrite sentences such as "Like, hey, dude, ah, yuh know, whoaah!" Even though that phrase has currency and unequivocal meaning in some circles, it conveys little scientifically to us.

- The "datum/data" controversy prompted the most responses to our September 1989 Comment; however, we shall cleave to the convention that *data are plural,* because instances arise where we need to retain the clear use of "datum," such as a topographic datum, a geodetic datum, an age datum, and a stratigraphic datum. Incidentally, *data show nothing.* It is the analyst's *interpretation* of the data that may yield some kind of a conclusion. Users of seismic reflection data tell us that many of those data "show" nothing unambiguously without interpretation.

- Jess Johnson compared "further" and "farther": "You wouldn't say 'I'm going fur away'; therefore 'far, farther, and farthest' for distance. The lawyer, when he finished cross examination, said 'no further questions'; it would sound strange to say 'no farther questions,' and so use 'further' in the context of 'additional.'" Dr. Johnson also admonished producers of manuscripts on word processors to proofread a hard copy rather than a screen. We agree from the nature of the errors we see on word-processed manuscripts and from our own experiences with them.

- Mason Hill pointed out that "faults do not move"; thus it is improper to talk about "fault movement" and how "a fault moved through time." Movement (of one block relative to another) may occur *along* a fault, a fault may offset something, and it is correct to talk about fault *displacement.*

- Amos Salvador maintained that "facies" is the most overworked and ambiguous term in the geological vocabulary. He pointed out that the *AGI Glossary of Geology* (1987) has seven different definitions of "facies." Without additional modifiers, such as "biofacies," "lithofacies," or "metamorphic facies," the term may be meaningless out of context. For that reason, Salvador recommended, and we concur, that the use of "facies" should be avoided if clarity of expression is desired.

- The use of "young" as a verb as in "the stratified sequence *youngs* to the west," is anathema to several stratigraphic readers. They and we prefer to say that "the stratified sequence is younger to the west." A nautical reader called attention to the fact that "westerly" is a nautical term; thus, geologists should say "the rocks were thrust *westward.*"

- We are still plagued by the indiscriminate overuse of "show," especially in figure captions. A recent example was "Map showing the geology of the Hardshell area" whereas "Geologic map of the Hardshell area" has always sufficed in the past. In this regard, we also consider it poor style to write first sentences of paragraphs such as: "Figure 5 shows the isotopic variations of basalt in the Hardshell area." The first sentence of a paragraph should introduce and even summarize the remainder of the paragraph. It should not be a description of the contents of a figure or repetition of what is already in the figure caption.

- So far, no one has offered definitions for "package," "packet," or "bundle" in the geologic context, or defended their use in preference to such good words as "bed," "stratum," "unit," "sequence," "block," "domain," "area," "region," and sundry other equally useful words.

- It is still distressing to see authors (and hear speakers) use "compression" for both stress and strain. Among rock mechanicists, "compression" is used only in the context of stress.

- Regrettably, it seems that the frequent use of "lithologies" as a synonym for "rocks" will die only when authors realize they do not say or write "geologies." Recently we saw that "Essentially four lithologies, each essentially composed of differing mineralogies, comprise the geologies essentially of four counties." Bah!

- "Superpose" has been preferred in place of "superimpose" since 1888, according to the AGI *Glossary,* because both words mean the same thing. The related word, "superimposition," has established usage largely in a geomorphic context in association with streams and glaciers. Otherwise, we prefer "superposition," in the stratigraphic and structural contexts. It sounds strange to talk about the "Principle of Superimposition."

- We see a creeping tendency to substitute "fabric" for "structure." This is improper, because *fabric* has always had a singular and historic connotation: "The *fabric* of an object is described by all of the spatial data *(fabric elements)* which it contains. A rock is said to have a *simple fabric* when it contains a single fabric element, such as lineation or foliation. A rock is said to have a *compound fabric* when it contains more than one fabric element, such as lineation or foliation" (with modification from Clark and McIntyre, 1951; see also Oertel, 1962). A fabric element is a penetrative structure on the scale of observation. A single fault is not a fabric element, although if it is one of a multitude of similarly oriented faults on the scale of a county or a state, then it is an element of the fabric defined by all of the faults.

- Why do authors, when submitting a manuscript for consideration for publication in the *Bulletin,* typically write in their cover letter: "Joe Schmoo and myself submit the enclosed manuscript. . . ."? Suppose Joe withdrew, then would the author have written "Myself submits the enclosed manuscript..."? We also see manuscripts "submitted by Joe Schmoo and *myself*" instead of "by Joe Schmoo and me." *Myself* is a reflexive pronoun and should be used only when "I" is the subject of the sentence.

- Watch and listen for the latest buzzword: "architecture." It is being used as a synonym for "structure," "geometry" (even "anatomy"), and diverse structural arrangements, including coils in molluscs ("the helicoidal internal architecture of *Helix pomata"),* the preferred orientation of *c* crystallographic axes in quartz ("the architecture of c-axes in the Hardshell quartzite"), the unconformable relations of strata ("the disparate stratal architecture between the Hardshell and Softshell Formation"), the variable attitudes of faults in a mountain range ("the crosscutting architecture of normal and reverse faults in the Hardshell area"), and collages of blocks on the continent scale ("the compressional architecture of Alaska"). Ugh!

Art Sylvester
John Costa

REFERENCES CITED

Bates, Robert L., and Jackson, Julia A., eds., 1987, *Glossary of geology* (3rd edition): Alexandria, Virginia, American Geological Institute, 788 p.

Clark, R.H., and McIntyre, D.B., 1951, A macroscopic method of fabric analysis: *American Journal of Science,* v. 249, p. 755-768.

Oertel, G., 1962, Extrapolation in geologic fabrics: *Geological Society of America Bulletin,* v. 73, p. 325-342.

The Science of Scientific Writing

In the November-December 1990 issue of *American Scientist* (3), George D. Gopen and Judith A. Swan make an excellent argument for improving scientific writing, and they lay down practical principles that will aid you as you write and revise your work. What follows is a considerably shortened summary of the article, reprinted here with the permission of *American Scientist,* journal of Sigma Xi, copyright © 1990 by Sigma Xi, The Scientific Research Society. I recommend the entire original article to all scientists and engineers.

Science is too often hard to read, but just because thoughts are complex does not mean that they must be difficult to comprehend. The fundamental purpose of scientific discourse is not the mere presentation of information and thought, but actual communication to a reader, and improving the quality of the writing also improves the quality of thought.

Readers do not simply read; they interpret. Because we read from left to right, and because we tend to read and interpret tabular information from left to right as well, we generally prefer the context for the "old" information to be on the left side (the beginning) of a sentence and the "new" information to be on the right side. Writing in this pattern of "old information on the left" and "new information on the right" meets a reader's natural expectations. In the same way that readers are misled or confused by too much experimental detail appearing in the "Results" section of a scientific report, too much "new information" on the left side of a sentence hinders reader comprehension and violates reader expectations.

Readers also have other expectations that good writers accommodate; they expect a grammatical subject to be followed soon after by a verb, and any intervening material between the subject and verb should supply information about the subject in an efficient and concrete manner.

Also, readers expect new, more complex information to fall in the "stress" position (the end) of the sentence. From all these expectations, the following principle arises for scientific writing:"

- "Put in the topic position the old information that links backward; put in the stress position the new information you want the reader to emphasize."

None of these reader-expectation principles should be considered "rules," but general maxims that will aid both writer and reader. There can be no fixed algorithm for good writing, because reader expectations are not the only guideposts writers use when composing, and because the best stylists are those who take the most original, creative approach.

With all this in mind, here are seven practical maxims to follow when writing in the sciences:

- Follow a grammatical subject as soon as possible with its verb.

- Place in the stress position the "new information" you want the reader to emphasize.

- Place the person or thing whose "story" a sentence is telling at the beginning of the sentence, in the topic position.

- Place appropriate "old information" (material already stated in the discourse) in the topic position for linkage backward and contextualization forward.

- Articulate the action of every clause or sentence in its verb.

- In general, provide context for your reader before asking that reader to consider anything new.

- In general, try to ensure that the relative emphases of the substance coincide with the relative expectations for emphasis raised by the structure.

Advice To Scientist-Writers: Beware Old 'Fallacies'

The following article appeared in the October 31, 1988, issue of *The Scientist* (4), and is reprinted with the permission of John Wiley & Sons, New York, copyright © 1988 by Henrietta J. Tichy. This article blasts away at the maxims that scientists have to struggle with whenever they write. Obsolete advice such as "essays are made up of five paragraphs" or "never end a sentence with a preposition" can ring in our ears and guide our writing habits for years, yet we always have far more options at our fingertips than any such rules suggest. The irony is that the very rules that guided us to become better writers are often the same ones that we have to shrug off or challenge as our writing matures. Because of our education and our quirky selective memories we often carry "writing fallacies" around with us that we must unlearn. So make a start on some good unlearning by reading the article that follows.

Bits of advice from fallacy land have a strong influence on writing. If cooking were controlled by such misconceptions, indigestion and poisoning would threaten at every meal. Unfortunately, scientists' writing has been poisoned by erring precepts that are no more accurate than a word passed around the circle is for the last listener.

Few people can concentrate on applying a dozen or more of these rigid rules without feeling so constrained that they hate to write. When they are forced to write, everything—diction, sentences, paragraphs—becomes awkward and unnatural, and every revision is made slowly and painfully. The best thing that scientist writers can do for themselves is to escape from the anxiety and strain caused by unnecessarily strict rules.

A good example of one such deadly rigid rule, "always use the passive voice," is a prescription so frequently pressed on writers of informational prose that it has proved to be one of the most harmful of all the fallacies. It is frequently enunciated by a person in a position superior to a writer's, such as a graduate school professor who insists that students write as the professors do—in the passive voice—in order to appear scholarly, to show objectivity, or to acquire a style like that of journal articles. Unfortunately, some writers have had poor advice impressed upon them so strongly that they cling to the misinformation tenaciously. (A consultant, late for an appointment with a foreign-born engineer who had learned English during his two years in the United States, apologized effusively. "It is nothing," the engineer replied courteously. "A cigarette was smoked and a book was read while waiting.")

Now, adroit use of the passive voice where it is suitable benefits style by permitting variations in meaning, stress, pace, and rhythm; but excessive use of the passive limits all components of expression. To write entirely in the passive would seem not just unwise but impossible; yet some misled scientists attempt it. The passive voice weakens style when it is used, consciously and unconsciously, to evade responsibility. One popular passive construction is "It is thought that…" When used anywhere in science and technology, the construction indicates that a general opinion or truth follows. But when scientist writers use it, they are likely to mean "I think that…," "we think that…," or even "I hope that somebody reading this thinks that…" Writers using these and other examples of "the evasive passive" run the risk of having their careful readers sound like hoot owls as they ask, "Who? Who? Who?"

The truth is, the active voice in most cases is much neater and briefer. "The safety committee recommended…" is better than "the recommendation was made by the safety committee…"

Another taboo, the rule against ending a sentence with a preposition, is a point about emphasis incorrectly applied. Near the end of an English sentence a major stress falls, sometimes on the last word, sometimes on a word just before the last word, sometimes on the final phrase. For effective emphasis, the word stressed should be important: "She said that she would complete the work on Monday." The stress is on *Monday.* Careful writers avoid stressing an unimportant word, like a preposition. But in many a sentence that ends with a preposition, the stress falls on the word before it. If that word is important, there is no need to rephrase the ending. Thus, it is acceptable to write "He is a difficult person to agree with" or "Children should have bright objects to play with."

Still another fallacy advises writers to avoid beginning sentences with certain words, such as "however," "but," and "and." There is a better way to approach this matter, still keeping in mind that the first word or words in a sentence are usually stressed, and they should indeed be important words. Occasionally even the much maligned *however* may be important because a writer wishes to emphasize that an unexpected shift in thought follows. *But* and *and,* which are also listed as forbidden first words by some teachers, seldom are stressed when they introduce a sentence. But they are often useful as unobtrusive initial conjunctions.

And then we have the harmful fallacy telling us to "avoid all personal pronouns. Never use *I* or *we."* First-person pronouns have long been absent from technical writing. They disappeared in the United States about 1920, when the impersonal style began to dominate in science and technology. (In the writing that comes out of the United States government—particularly from the Pentagon—*I* and *we* or any other indication that a human being is writing are taboo.) However, an attempt to achieve objectivity by avoiding personal pronouns is a mistake, and the idea that using the third person instead of the first person achieves modesty is equally wrong. Discarding necessary words like *I* and *we* merely leads to awkward writing marked by excessive use of the passive and by reliance on weak indirect constructions. Writers deprived of *I* and *we* turn to unnatural and objectionable substitutes: *the author, one, the present writer, this reporter,* and so forth. Sometimes, avoiding the use of the first person in an effort to sound modest backfires. Consider the sentence "The national secretary of the society initiated the following improvements in the management of the central office." This sounds far more immodest than the simply stated "I initiated the following improvements…"

Today, prohibition of the first person is obsolete, although writers should avoid constantly using it. Most scientific and technical journals now permit authors to use *I* for a single writer and *we* for more than one writer, especially when the material is personal, as in interpretation of results and in predictions. Indeed, many editors urge this use whenever appropriate. The *American National Standard for the Preparation of Scientific Papers for Written or Oral Presentation* states, "When a verb concerns action by the author, the first person should be used, especially in matters of experimental design ('To eliminate this possibility, I did the following experiment')."

Half a century or so ago, when the personal pronouns and active voice were reduced to a minimum or eliminated, much writing on science and technology became lifeless and dull. This led to the fallacy that writing on professional subjects has to be dull and that there is no use trying to do anything about it. However, in my experience there is a marked correlation between the excellence of writers' understanding of a subject and the clarity and grace of their written thoughts on it.

Indeed, many major businesses and industries are pressing hard for readable prose from their scientists. To achieve it, good writers and editors have been freeing themselves from unnecessary rules and regulations. Instead of droning *never use the active voice* and *never use personal pronouns*, they have been concentrating on the functions of the active and passive voices, on the functions of personal and impersonal pronouns, and on the avoidance of usage and style not suited to the idiom of the English language. It will be interesting to watch the changes that occur.

The Universal Recipe For Scientific Reports

What follows is a reprint of an article that anyone who ever writes a scientific report or submits an article to a journal simply must read and use. From the sharp mind of a seasoned editor, this article gives us an inside track on just what editors are looking for when they select scientific articles for publication. This article is the best I have seen at what it does, and is made more enjoyable by the editor's wit, examples, and exactitude. From the entertaining title of the original article—"The Universal Recipe, Or How To Get Your Manuscript Accepted By Persnickety Editors" (5)—to the gracious closing acknowledgments, we see again that editors are people too (some, I suspect, even ride mountain bikes and keep pets). This article is reprinted with the kind permission of the author, copyright © 1990 by The Clay Minerals Society.

THE RECIPE

Overview
Despite the enormous diversity of the many branches of science and technology, the manner of reporting scientific and technical information seems to have resolved itself over the years into a rather standard format—a format that appears to be just about the same regardless of the particular area of science being discussed. This format has emerged by trial and error and today seems to be the most universally accepted means of conveying scientific ideas and information. Although minor variations may be found, the standard format or recipe for acceptable manuscripts consists of the following major parts:

1. Title
2. Authorship
3. Abstract
4. Introduction
5. Experimental (or Methods & Materials)
6. Results
7. Discussion
8. Conclusions (or Summary & Conclusions)
9. Acknowledgments
10. References Cited

At this point, a few readers of this article will undoubtedly say to themselves that this standard format or recipe is all well and good for most papers and for most authors, but "my" work is different and therefore "my" manuscript should be organized in a "different" or "special" way. In answer, this editor says "not so," or at least not so for 99.99% of the manuscripts he has ever dealt with. Rarely does a scientific investigation require a reporting style that differs substantially from this standard format. Granted, some manuscripts may benefit by a separate Theory section or Theoretical Background section (probably inserted after the Introduction), or a Regional Geology section (inserted either before or after the Experimental section), or even an extended Literature Review section (inserted after the Introduction), but the presence of such extra sections does not change the overall organization of the manuscript, nor do such sections detract (if they are properly written) from a straightforward, "eins, zwei, drei" manner of presentation. The standard format or universal recipe allows authors to tell the reader specifically what problem they attempted to solve (Introduction), how they went about solving it (Experimental section), what they found out (Results), and how they interpreted these results (Discussion). It also allows them to tell the reader something about the significance of their findings (Summary and Conclusions).

The key to writing an acceptable scientific paper is organization. Most editors, technical referees, and critical readers agree that disorganized writing may reflect a disorganized investigation, and a disorganized investigation is tantamount to a poor investigation, of little use to anyone. This editor strongly suggests that authors organize their reports into the standard format here. I also recommend that authors prepare extended hierarchical outlines of their reports before they put pen to paper (or finger to keyboard). I recognize that many authors do not need outlines before they write, but as a minimum I suggest that their final manuscripts be reduced to outline form as soon as they are completed. In this way any lack of organization becomes readily apparent.

The major sections of such an outline are, of course, the major sections of the universal recipe. These sections are discussed below in terms of the purpose, the kind of information that should or should not be reported, and the pitfalls that should be avoided in preparing each section. Although I would like to claim them as my own, few of the ideas expressed here originate with this editor. Almost all are well discussed in numerous books on technical or scientific writing, some of which are listed at the end of this article. I strongly urge all authors or potential authors to read or re-read one or more of these works and to refer to them constantly as they prepare their next manuscript.

Title

The title of a scientific paper should tell the reader what the paper is all about. It should not be too short or too general (the title of Theophrastus' treatise "On Stones" would be considered inadequate today), or too long (the title "Unit-Cell Dimensions of Potassium Feldspar in Early to Middle Pleistocene Rocks of Southeastern North Dakota as a Function of Alkali Element Composition of Circulating Ground Waters and of Organic Carbon Content of Overlying Lignitic Shales" might put the readers to sleep before they get into the body of the paper). Because everyone who picks up the journal will undoubtedly read the title of the paper, the title is the author's first chance (and maybe the only chance) to tell the readers what the paper is all about and thereby convince them to read on.

In addition to being not-too-long and not-too-short, the title should tell the reader just what will be covered in the paper. It should not give the reader the impression that an entire field will be treated in the paper when in reality only a small part of that field is discussed. Thus, the title "Adsorption of Amino Acids on Kaolinite in Ethyl Alcohol" is more informative than "Amino Acid-Kaolinite Reactions." Moreover, words that do not contribute specifically to the subject of the paper have no place in the title. For example, the first four words of the title "Preliminary Results on the Effect of Magnesium in the Formation of Chlorite" add nothing, and the title is better written "Effect of Magnesium in Chlorite Formation." The title also should not be an alphabet soup of abbreviations or acronyms, many of which may not be understood by the non-expert reader.

Authorship

Authorship of technical papers is a delicate subject and one that most editors are happy to avoid. For the most part, the individuals to be listed as authors and the order in which they are listed should be settled well before the manuscript is submitted for publication. From an editorial point of view, however, a few comments are in order. First, it is perplexing to see long lists of individuals named as the authors of a technical paper, even in this age of cooperative or group research. Lengthy lists of authors suggest unresolved problems of laboratory politics, rather than accurate accounts of the principal contributors to the work at hand. Conversely, some works appear to cry out for additional authors, especially those that draw heavily on student theses or that are based on unpublished information obtained from another party. Hence, the list of authors should include the principal contributors to the project; those who participated in the project in a peripheral manner or only briefly should not be forgotten, but recognized with appreciation in the Acknowledgments section. I will not attempt to state what is an acceptable number of authors, but merely state that credibility decreases as the number increases beyond five or six. Nor will I spell out specifically the meaning of "principal contributor" or "peripheral manner," but leave interpretation of these somewhat ambiguous terms to the authors (or potential authors) themselves.

One subject concerning authorship does merit serious consideration, and that is that *all* authors of a paper are responsible for the content of that paper. If a particular coauthor does not agree with what has been said in the paper, that coauthor should divorce himself or herself from that paper. In this regard, the principal author (generally the writer) should make sure that *all* authors of the paper have an opportunity to review, criticize, and contribute to the preparation of the manuscript before it is submitted for publication and before it is resubmitted after having been revised to address the referees' comments. Fulfilling this obligation in itself should drastically limit the number of authors.

Abstract

Not enough can be said about the importance of the Abstract. With the exception of the Title itself, more people will read the Abstract than any other part of the paper. In this era of megapublications, few researchers have time to read everything, even in their own fields of specialization. I am loathe to admit it, but the editor is probably the only person who reads every word of every article in each issue of a given journal. Most of us scan the titles in the table of contents and then turn to the abstracts of the papers that seem to be of interest. If the abstract turns out to be uninformative (i.e., if it really doesn't summarize the highlights of the paper), or if it is merely a table of contents of what is to be found in the rest of the paper, most of us will grumble a little about authors who try to keep their findings secret and probably move on to *another* paper.

Only the true expert or avid lover of the subject will read the entire paper, and these people will read it regardless of how well or how poorly the abstract is written. It is therefore not for the expert in the subject that authors prepare informative abstracts—it is for everyone else who might read them. Because most of these non-experts will not read beyond the abstract, it is vital that authors convey everything they can about the paper—the rationale for undertaking the investigation, the important findings (including specific data, rather than arm-waving generalities), and the pertinent interpretations of those findings—in the abstract. In short, the abstract should be a fact-filled condensation of the entire paper. Many editors and reviewers take the attitude that if a subject is not of such significance as to be summarized in the abstract, perhaps it does not belong in the main body of the paper either.

Note that in the above discussion I haven't said that abstracts are easy to prepare. They are not. For me at least, the abstract is the most difficult part of the manuscript, chiefly because I am forced to condense each part of the paper into a sentence or two and to construct those sentences with great care so that each contains the maximum amount of information. The author part of me says that surely my colleagues will want to read my wonderful paper in its entirety, and, therefore, I don't have to tell them everything in the abstract, but the editor part of me knows differently; hence, if I want the maximum number of people to benefit from or be aware of the results of my investigation, I must make sure that the abstract says as much as possible.

To illustrate the difference between uninformative and informative abstracts, I recommend reading the abstracts in the program of some past scientific conference and *then* reading the abstracts of these same papers as they are published in the conference proceedings or in a primary journal, after a persnickety editor and a couple of referees have had a chance to work on them.

Introduction

Magazine advertisements and television commercials must arouse interest in the first few words—otherwise the audience will turn the page or go to the kitchen for a cold beer. Likewise, the Introduction of a scientific paper must in a few short sentences convince the reader that it is worthwhile to read on. The Introduction must set the stage for the paper to follow and convey to the reader the rationale for undertaking the investigation. It should spell out the specific objectives of the investigation and describe the nature and scope of the problem, why that problem is important, how the author attempted to solve that problem, and of what significance are the results that the author expected to obtain. Some Introductions also mention *very briefly* the principal findings of the investigation, so as not to keep the reader in suspense until the Conclusions. If all these questions are addressed in the

Introduction, the reader will know what to expect in the rest of the paper. Authors must recognize that their scientific results may be of enormous significance and that their interpretations may be truly awe-inspiring, but if readers cannot grasp why the investigation was conducted in the first place, they may never bother to read about these wonderful results or these revolutionary conclusions.

The Introduction is generally the place to review the literature, at least to the extent of demonstrating how the present investigation relates to past work. Every paper ever written on the subject, however, need not be mentioned; the author should cite only those papers that bear directly on the problem to be attacked in the present investigation. Authors should also be careful to indicate exactly why a particular work was cited and exactly how the cited work relates to the subject under discussion. It is frustrating, for example, to read in the Introduction of a paper on "Hydrolysis of Manganese During the Weathering of Ultramafic Rocks" that "Jones and Smith (1978) noted manganese hydroxides in weathered serpentinites." I sometimes want almost to shake the author to learn what it was that Jones and Smith found out about manganese hydroxides in such rocks or what Jones and Smith discussed that is germane to the problem being investigated in the present paper.

Authors should also avoid citing the literature for information that is common knowledge. I once noted the statement in the Introduction to a paper submitted to *Clays and Clay Minerals* that "Clay minerals are abundant in sedimentary rocks and soils (Grim, 1953)." Such information was, of course, mentioned in the cited work, but was it really necessary for the author to cite Professor Grim's book—or any published work for that matter—for such common knowledge? On the other hand, because one of the purposes of the Introduction is to show the reader how the present investigation meshes with or fills a gap in our current knowledge, authors should not overlook important works on the same subject by other researchers. Even if the author doesn't agree with them, fairness requires that other points of view be recognized and considered. Furthermore, simply because an important work happens to be published in a language not understood by the author is no excuse not to include it in the review of the literature.

Well-written Introductions invariably end with what many have called a "succinct statement of the problem." Here, in one or two sentences the author should state precisely what the rest of the paper will be about and, perhaps, exactly what will be shown as a result of the investigation. For example, the closing statement in the Introduction to the paper on the hydrolysis of manganese mentioned above might be: "To investigate the hydrolysis reactions of manganese during the weathering of ultramafic rocks, samples of fresh serpentinite and peridotite were treated with weak acids at room temperature for periods ranging from weeks to years. Reactions were followed by analyzing solid products and residual solutions and plotting the results on appropriate Eh-pH diagrams." The "statement of the problem" at the end of the Introduction is therefore analogous to a speaker saying: "I've told you what subject I'm going to discuss, and I've told you why that subject is important. Now I'm going to give you specific details on the subject and then my interpretation of them. Pay attention—you don't want to miss what's coming next!"

Experimental section

The Experimental section of any scientific paper is probably the easiest to write and is often the first section to be tackled by the author. It is no less important, however, than any other section, inasmuch as a basic criterion of scientific publishing is that the reader be able to duplicate an author's results using the same procedures. The Experimental section should therefore be a straightforward presentation of what materials were used in the investigation (reagents, rock, water, soil, or mineral samples), how these materials were treated (chemically, thermally, electrically), how starting materials and products were characterized (by X-ray powder diffraction, nuclear magnetic resonance, infrared spectroscopy, optical microscopy, transmission electron microscopy, or extended X-ray absorption fine-structure spectroscopy), and how the data were "massaged" and evaluated (statistically, mathematically).

The locality, source, and properties of all starting samples should be reported in as much detail as possible to allow the reader to compare the author's results with other data reported previously on the "same" material. In so far as the locality is concerned, note, for example, that "Germany" hardly suffices as a precise locality of a nontronite from Clausthal-Zellerfeld, Federal Republic of Germany. Samples obtained from reference collections, e.g., from the Source Clay Repository of The Clay Minerals Society, should be so indicated and designated with their assigned reference numbers. Standard methods used should be referenced, but need not be described in detail; however, new methods or modifications of standard methods should be described in as much detail as necessary to allow them to be used by the readers. The brand name and model of the instruments used should be stated, not as an endorsement of that product, but so that the reader can evaluate the quality of the data being reported. The precision of all measurements should be stated, and the statistical methods and computer programs used to evaluate the data should be identified and referenced.

Except as they add to the characterization of the starting materials or samples, results generally should not be reported in the Experimental section.

Results section

Despite the fact that many *authors* find it convenient to combine the experimental results obtained by a particular technique or on a particular suite of samples and an interpretation of these results in the same section, most *readers* find it extremely difficult to follow a paper written in this manner. The reader generally wants to see the results of the investigation neatly presented in a separate section, unencumbered by discussion, interpretation, or comparison with the literature. The reader would *then* like to see the author's interpretations of these results in a separate section. In this way, the author's new data can be distinguished from information that is common knowledge or that has been reported by earlier workers. Although a few papers lend themselves to combining results and discussion in the same section, most do not, and, in general, interpretations and discussions should be presented in a section separate from Results.

The results themselves should be presented preferably in tables or as curves, graphs, or halftone illustrations. Details of experimental procedures should not be included in the Results section, but gathered together in the Experimental section, as noted above. Descriptions of the results should be as brief as possible and devoid of interpretation, although particular trends or ranges of the data should be pointed out. Some authors believe that because certain information was obtained in the course of their investigation, this information should be reported in their paper regardless of whether it is germane to the subject under discussion. Only those results relevant to the purpose of the paper, however, should be reported. Extraneous data, fascinating as the authors might find them, should be saved for another day and another paper.

Editors frequently encounter manuscripts that present exciting new experimental techniques, in which samples from several unrelated subject areas have been tested to demonstrate the universality of the method. Unfortunately the authors of many of these papers have tried to address major *research problems* on the basis of these new, but limited results in this same paper. The net result is that the major contribution, i.e., the new experimental technique, all but gets lost in the shuffle, and the authors do a woefully inadequate job with respect to the research problems. The moral of the tale is to limit a manuscript to a single subject and not try to solve all of the world's problems in a single paper. Use these preliminary data to begin a whole new investigation.

Discussion section

The Discussion is probably the most important section of the paper and should be carefully organized into specific subsections, each dealing with a different subject. In each subsection, the author should critically evaluate the data, show how they agree or contrast with published works, and interpret them for the reader. It is not sufficient for the author to point towards a table or graph and expect the readers to interpret the data themselves; the author must do the interpreting and, in so doing, must solidly base these interpretations on specific data reported in the present paper or on a combination of published information and current results.

Technical reviewers and editors have a habit of downgrading manuscripts if interpretations are not (or do not appear to be) strongly supported by data reported in the paper. All too often, authors make sweeping statements or draw broad conclusions without telling the reader specifically on which data these statements or conclusions have been based. Others merely refer the reader to "the data in Table 1" or to "the results reported above," and some only say "therefore" or "thus" as a means of specifying the data on which conclusions are based. Such tactics leave the reader wondering whether or not the author truly has evidence to support these statements or if the statements are more wishful thinking than data-based interpretations.

Authors should keep in mind that readers are not obliged to believe what they are told, but they will be more inclined to do so if they are provided with specific results and evidence every step of the way. Therefore, authors should present their specific data or information on which a conclusion will be drawn *first* in a sentence or paragraph in the Discussion section, and *then* discuss or interpret these data. Nothing is quite so annoying as being presented with what appears to be a statement of fact and then having to read on to discover the data on which the statement was based.

Many papers phrase all statements and discussion in the present tense, leaving the readers to determine for themselves whether the statements refer to the author's present findings or to facts already known. No hard and fast rules apply, but, in this editor's opinion, the author's results are best described in the past tense, reserving the present tense for information currently known or for information taken from the literature. Objects still possessing particular properties or characteristics, however, may properly be described in the present tense. For example, an author describing a rock sample might write that "The rock *is* red and *has* a granitoid texture," but that its density *"was* determined to be 3.00 g/cm3"; likewise, that the "bands characteristic of Al-O bonding *were noted* in the infrared spectrum," but that the "infrared spectrum in Figure 3 *shows* bands characteristic of Al-O bonding."

Conclusions (or Summary and Conclusions) section
Authors often confuse "Summary" with "Conclusions." A Summary section by definition sums up the results and interpretations of the paper, and, in some degree, may duplicate part of the Abstract. In some papers, the results of the investigation and the discussion of them are summarized in a final subsection of the Discussion; in others, a separate section is warranted, usually combined with Conclusions.

A Conclusions section is the section in which authors should discuss the importance of their findings. The conclusions should not merely repeat various points of the discussion, but should tell the reader *why* these points are important, something about their broad meaning, how they contribute to our understanding of the field being examined, and where more work is needed. A combined Summary and Conclusions section may be the appropriate place to summarize the findings of the investigation and to point out their overall significance.

As an author prepares the Summary and Conclusions section of the manuscript, the Introduction should be reexamined, especially the part in which the objectives of the investigation were spelled out, to see whether or not these objectives have been met. If they have not been met, the author should tell the reader why not, or should consider rewriting the Introduction to contain a different set of objectives.

Acknowledgments section
Although a necessary part of any scientific paper, the Acknowledgments section should be brief and to the point. It is only proper to recognize individuals and institutions that contributed financial support, samples, specific analyses, and technical assistance to the investigation, however, thanking everyone whom the author has ever been associated with over the last 20 years, like an Academy Award acceptance speech, is inappropriate. Unquestionably, the individuals who critiqued the manuscript before it was sent to a journal and the referees (identified and anonymous) who reviewed it for the journal should

be acknowledged with appreciation. The journal editor need not be thanked, because everyone knows what a wonderful job this person does all the time.

References Cited section

Little can be said about the References Cited section, except that authors should submit their list of references cited in the *exact* style of the journal, down to the last jot and tittle of punctuation, spacing, etc. I am painfully aware that every journal has its own style, and wouldn't it be nice if they all used the same style, but they don't, and that's a fact of life that authors must live with. Keep in mind that editors will insist that authors follow the prescribed style of the journal, so why not do it right the first time? Most journals spell out the style to be used in their Instructions to Authors. If such instructions are not available, authors are advised to examine a recent issue of the journal in question to see how it's done.

In general, only works that have actually been published (or, perhaps, that have been formally accepted for publication by a journal) should be listed in the references. All others should be cited in the body of the text in the form of a personal (or written) communication, which includes the full name, institution, and current address of the individual from whom the information was obtained. Such information is necessary to allow the reader to communicate directly with that individual for clarification, verification, or further information. Authors should also check the final manuscript to make sure that each item in the list of references has actually been cited in the text and that each citation in the text is listed in the References Cited section.

RECAPITULATION

These ideas for the ideal manuscript for publication in *Clays and Clay Minerals* or for any other technical journal are offered to help authors write reports of their investigations that will be read, understood, and appreciated by their colleagues. No matter how great the experiment or how revolutionary the results, nothing is added to that vast accumulation of information we call science, if the author's work is not published or if it is published and still cannot be understood. Even worse, mankind reaps no benefit. My discussion has concentrated only on the main parts of a "Universal Recipe" for scientific manuscripts. In the final analysis, no two papers are exactly alike, and authors may wish to modify the universal recipe (but not too much) to fit each investigation.

The final word. Every manuscript submitted for publication should be critically reviewed by a third party who can be depended on to "tell it like it is." Authors should not submit manuscripts that represent anything less than their very best efforts, and critical reviews by colleagues for both technical content and manner of presentation are a vital part of the manuscript-preparation process. Remember, dear author, the sole purpose of a scientific paper is to convey information in a succinct and unambiguous manner, and the data and discussion must be presented in concise, understandable statements. Anything that gets in the way of fulfilling this purpose—flowery prose, personal "style," imprecise words, tortuous sentence structure, or jargon-filled paragraphs—must be ruthlessly deleted from the manuscript by the author. Don't make the referees or the editor do this for you.

Raw, unreviewed manuscripts, best described as "rough drafts," place an excessive burden on the journal, its editor, and its technical referees. Many of the questions raised by the referees could probably have been answered beforehand by the authors if they had only asked a colleague to review their papers. Internal or external review prior to submission of the manuscript to a journal is an excellent means of catching poor organization, verbose explanations, convoluted reasoning, unwarranted interpretations, and unsupported conclusions. It also speeds up publication of that world-class paper we all strive to produce.

MY ACKNOWLEDGMENTS

I am grateful to past and present associate editors of *Clays and Clay Minerals* and to dozens of other scientific and editorial colleagues for their comments over the years about the need for and means of achieving good writing in scientific papers. R.A. Sheppard and Diane Schnabel of the U.S. Geological Survey, Denver, Colorado, significantly improved my "unimprovable" first draft. The following texts on technical writing focused my own thoughts on this subject and provided a base for the present note, especially Robert A. Day's *How to Write and Publish a Scientific Paper.*

SELECTED TEXTS ON TECHNICAL WRITING

Barnett, M.T. (1974) *Elements of Technical Writing:* Delmar Publishers, Albany, New York, 232 pp.

Bishop, E.E., Eckel, E.B., and Others (1978) *Suggestions to Authors of the Reports of the United States Geological Survey:* 6th ed., U.S. Government Printing Office, Washington D.C., 273 pp.

Day, R.A. (1983) *How to Write and Publish a Scientific Paper:* 2nd ed., ICI Press, Philadelphia, Pennsylvania, 181 pp.

Dodd, Janet S., ed. (1986) *The ACS Style Guide: A Manual for Authors and Editors:* American Chemical Society, Washington D.C., 264 pp.

Hayes, Robert (1965) *Principles of Technical Writing:* Addison-Wesley, Menlo Park, California, 324 pp.

Hoover, Hardy (1980) *Essentials for the Scientific and Technical Writer:* Dover Publications, New York, 216 pp.

Katz, M.J. (1985) *Elements of a Scientific Paper:* Yale University Press, New Haven, Connecticut, 130 pp.

Tichy, H.J. (1966) *Effective Writing for Engineers, Managers, Scientists:* Wiley, New York, 337 pp.

A Bibliography Of Additional Journal Articles About Writing

Across the country, writing-across-the-curriculum courses and programs are burgeoning, and, as the articles in this chapter illustrate, there have long been cries for better writing in the sciences and engineering from supervisors, teachers, and editors. Loosely, writing-across-the-curriculum can be defined as a commitment by academic programs to incorporate a substantial amount of writing into specialized courses within a student's major; the writing-across-the-curriculum philosophy embraces the use of writing as a way to teach course content in every classroom where it is feasible to do so.

Writing-across-the-curriculum is not a new concept, but it has grown enormously in the past decade. As a complement to the material in this chapter, I offer you a brief bibliography of additional articles from specialized journals and textbooks that share the concept that writing can and should be used as a learning tool outside of composition courses. Of course there are many articles on writing-across-the-curriculum in rhetoric and composition journals, but the articles most appropriate for the users of this manual come from specialized journals outside of rhetoric and composition. This bibliography—which includes over 60 articles—is just a small sample of articles from the technical journals and textbooks that view writing as a tool for learning about a field.

Anatomy and Physiology

Squitieri, Louise. Cue: How to Get Started Writing in Anatomy and Physiology, *Journal of College Science Teaching.* 17(4):279-280, 326; Feb. 1988.

Biology

Ambron, Joanna. Writing to Improve Learning in Biology, *Journal of College Science Teaching.* 16(4):263-266; Feb. 1987.

Dunn, James R. Improving the Vocabulary and Writing Skills of Black Students Majoring in Biology, *Journal of College Science Teaching.* 17(5):360-363; March/April 1988.

Ryan, Janet N. The Secret Language of Science or, Radicals in the Classroom, *The American Biology Teacher.* 47(2):91; Feb. 1985.

TePaske, E. Russell. Writing in Biology: One Way to Improve Analytical Thinking, *The American Biology Teacher.* 44(2):98-99; Feb. 1982.

Wandersee, James. Are There Too Many Terms to Learn in Biology? *The American Biology Teacher.* 47(6):346-347; Sept. 1985.

Business

Crosser, Rick and Laufer, Doug. The "Writing Across the Curriculum" Concept in Accounting and Tax Courses, *Journal of Education For Business.* 66(2):83-87; Nov./Dec. 1990.

Chemistry

Adamson, Ishola. An Appraisal of a New Undergraduate Biochemistry Research Project, *Journal of Chemical Education.* 57(3):180; March 1980.

Bailey, David N. and Markowicz, Leon. Chemistry and English: A New Bond, *Journal of Chemical Education.* 60(6):467-468; June 1983.

Bean, John C. and Goodman, W. Daniel. A Chemistry Laboratory Project to Develop Thinking and Writing Skills, *Journal of Chemical Education.* 60(6):483-484; June 1983.

Eisenberg, Anne. Strategies Five Productive Chemists Use to Handle the Writing Process, *Journal of Chemical Education.* 59(7):566-569; July 1982.

Fulwiler, Toby and Strauss, Michael J. Interactive Writing and Learning Chemistry, *Journal of College Science Teaching.* 15(4):256-262; Feb. 1987.

Leesley, M.E. and Williams, M.L. Improving the Writing of Freshman Chemical Engineers, *Engineering Education.* 69(4):337-339; Jan. 1979.

Malachowski, Mitchell R. Honing Observation Skills by the Use of Writing Exercises, *Journal of Chemical Education.* 63(6):497; June 1986.

Melhado, L. Lee. Chemical Composition: Improving the Writing and Literature

Search Skills of Students in the Chemical Sciences, *Journal of Chemical Education*. 57(2):127-128; Feb. 1980.

Melhado, L. Lee. Technical Writing and the Chemical Literature: A Unified Approach, *Journal of College Science Teaching*. 10(5):299-302; March 1981.

Zimmerman, S. Scott. Writing For Chemistry: Food For Thought Must be Appetizing, *Journal of Chemical Education*. 55(11):727; Nov. 1978.

Engineering

Covington, David H. and Krowne, Clifford M. A Survey of Technical Communication Students: Some Implications For Engineering Educators, *Engineering Education*. 73(3):247-251; Dec. 1982.

Feuerstein, Irwin A., and Woods, Donald R. On Teaching Technical Communication, *Engineering Education*. 70(7):745-749; April 1980.

Friday, Chet. An Evaluation of Graduating Engineers' Writing Proficiency, *Engineering Education*. 77(2):114-116; Nov. 1986.

Kiyama, Ken and Nold, Ellen. Engineering Students Teach Each Other to Write, *Engineering Education*. 69(4):334-337; Jan. 1979.

Klaver, Peter, Mathes, J.C., and Stevenson, Dwight W. Technical Communication: The Engineering Educator's Responsibility, *Engineering Education*. 69(4):331-334; Jan. 1979.

Pfeiffer, William S. Engineering Proposals: Teaching Students the Basics, *Engineering Education*. 76(2):109-111; Nov. 1985.

Reed, Joseph R. Writing Potential of Engineers: Underdeveloped? *Engineering Education*. 73(3):260; Dec. 1982.

Sides, Charles H. What Should We Do With Technical Writing? *Engineering Education*. 70(7):743-744; April 1980.

Skerl, Jennie. A Writing Center For Engineering Students, *Engineering Education*. 70(7):752-755; April 1980.

Sylvester, Nicholas D. Engineering Education Must Improve the Communication Skills of Its Graduates, *Engineering Education*. 70(7):739-740; April 1980.

Tebeaux, Elizabeth. Technical Writing Is Not Enough, *Engineering Education*. 70(7):741-743; April 1980.

Wilcox, Sidney W. Communication Courses for Engineering Students, *Engineering Education*. 70(7):750-752; April 1980.

Mathematics

Connolly, Paul and Vilardi, Teresa, eds. *Writing to Learn Mathematics and Science*. New York: Teachers College, Columbia University. 1989. 307 pp.

Geeslin, William E. Using Writing About Mathematics as a Teaching Technique, *The Mathematics Teacher*. 70(2):112-115; Feb, 1977.

Gopen, George D. and Smith, David A. What's an Assignment Like You Doing in a Course Like This?: Writing to Learn Mathematics, *The College Mathematics Journal*. 21(1):2-19; Jan. 1990.

King, Barbara. Using Writing in the Mathematics Class: Theory and Practice, *New Directions For Teaching and Learning: No. 12. Teaching Writing in All Disciplines*, Griffin, C. Williams, ed. San Francisco: Josey-Bass, Inc. 1982.

Norris, Eugene M. and Paik, Minja K. Writing to Learn in Statistics, Mathematics, and Computer Science: Two Views, *Writing To Learn: Essays and Reflections on Writing Across the Curriculum*. Thaiss,

Christopher, ed. Dubuque, Iowa: Kendall/Hunt Publishing Company. pp. 107-111. 1983.

Norris, Eugene M. Writing in Math and Computer Science, *Writing To Learn: Essays and Reflections on Writing Across the Curriculum.* Thaiss, Christopher, ed. Dubuque, Iowa: Kendall/Hunt Publishing Company. pp. 112-115. 1983.

Senk, Sharon L. How Well Do Students Write Geometry Proofs? *Mathematics Teacher.* 78(6):448-456; Sept. 1985.

Watson, Margaret. Writing Has a Place in a Mathematics Class, *The Mathematics Teacher.* 73(7):518-519; Oct. 1980.

Music

Beaty, Dan and Schoenewolf, C.R. A Marriage of English and Music, *Music Educator's Journal.* 59(7):64-65; March 1973.

Oliphant, Robert. Music and Language: A New Look at an Old Analogy, *Music Educator's Journal.* 58(7):60-63; March 1972.

Winston, Edmund W. Three Rs & an M, *Music Educator's Journal.* 69(4):40; Dec. 1982.

Nursing/Medicine

DeBakey, Lois and Debakey, Selma, eds. Muddy Medical Writing: Is the Culprit 'Bad Grammar,' Technical Terminology, or Undisciplined Reasoning? *Southern Medical Journal.* 69(10):1253-1254; Oct. 1976.

King, Lester S. Better Writing Anyone? (editorial), *Journal of the American Medical Association.* 239(8):752; Feb. 20, 1978.

Shephard, David A.E. Accuracy, Brevity, Clarity: Three Principles of Good Medical Writing (letter to editor), *Anesthesia and Analgesia.* 55(6):893-894; Nov./Dec. 1976.

Sorrell, Jeanne Merkle. Mentoring Students in Writing: 'Gourmet Express' Versus 'Fast Food Service,' *Journal of Nursing Education.* 30(6):284-286; June 1991.

Physics

Arons, Arnold B. Thinking, Reasoning, and Understanding in Introductory Physics Courses, *The Physics Teacher.* 19(3):166-172; March1981.

Cook, Gayl P. Grading Labs: The Self-Checking Questionnaire, *The Physics Teacher.* 23(2):95-97; Feb. 1985.

Davies, Brian. Physics Lectures and Student Notes, *Physics Education.* 11(1):33-36; Jan. 1976.

Greenslade, Thomas B., Jr. An Alternate Form of Examination Question, *The Physics Teacher.* 23(3):160; March 1985.

Jewett, John W., Jr. Learning Introductory Physics Through Required Writing Assignments, *Journal of College Science Teaching.* 21(1):20-25; Sept./Oct. 1991.

Kirkpatrick, Larry D. and Pittendrigh, Adele S. A Writing Teacher in the Physics Classroom, *The Physics Teacher.* 22(3):159-164; March 1984.

Payne, Mark W. Required Careful Writing (letter to editor), *The Physics Teacher.* 22(5):278; May 1984.

Richmond, P.E. Writing About Physics, *Physics Education.* 15(6):361-363; Nov. 1980.

Sociology

Day, Susan. Producing Better Writers in Sociology Classes: A Test of the

Writing Across the Curriculum Approach, *Teaching Sociology.* 17(4):458-464; Oct. 1989.

Jobes, Patrick C. and Pittendrigh, Adele S. Teaching Across the Curriculum: Critical Communication in the Sociology Classroom, *Teaching Sociology.* 11(3):281-296; April 1984.

Nath Kalia, Narendra. The Sociological Book Review: A Substitute for the Standard Term Paper, *Teaching Sociology.* 11(2):213-217; Jan. 1984.

Singh, Raghu N. and Unnithan, N. Prabha. Free to Write: On the Use of Speculative Writing in Sociology Classes, *Teaching Sociology.* 17(4):465-470; Oct. 1989.

Writing in the Sciences and Engineering in General

Brillhart, L.V. and Debs, M.B. Teaching Writing—A Scientist's Responsibility, *Journal Of College Science Teaching.* 10(5):303-304; March 1981.

Feinberg, Susan. Feedback on Format Improves Technical Writing, *Engineering Education.* 69(4):339-342; Jan. 1979.

Foos, K. Michael. Abstracts Can Enhance Writing Skills, *Journal of College Science Teaching.* 16(4):254-255; Feb. 1987.

Griffin, C. Williams, ed. *New Directions For Teaching and Learning: No. 12. Teaching Writing in All Disciplines.* San Francisco: Josey-Bass, Inc. 1982. 93 pp.

Madigan, Chris. Writing as a Means, Not an End, *Journal of College Science Teaching.* 16(4):245-249; Feb. 1987.

Mertens, Thomas R. Reflections on Writing and Reviewing Grant Proposals, *Journal of College Science Teaching.* 16(4):267-269; Feb. 1987.

Potera, Carol. The Basic Elements of Writing a Scientific Paper: The Art of Scientific Style, *Journal of Chemical Education.* 61(3):246-248; March 1984.

Spears, James E. A Simulated Writing Experience, *Engineering Education.* 69(4):342-344; Jan. 1979.

References Cited

INTRODUCTION

1. 631-636; 1990. Chandler, Harry E.. *The "How to Write What" Book.* Ohio: American Society of Metals. p. 5. 1979.
2. Davis, Richard M. How Important is Technical Writing?—A Survey of Opinions of Successful Engineers, *The Technical Writing Teacher.*:83-88. 1977.
3. Lampe, David R. Engineer's Invisible Activity: Writing, *Technology Review.* 86(3):73-74; April 1983.
4. Sylvester, Nicholas D. Engineering Education Must Improve the Communication Skills of Its Graduates, *Engineering Education.* 70(7):739-740; April 1980.
5. Bohren, Craig F. 1991. Excerpted from an unpublished letter to *Science News* magazine. Dr. Craig Bohren, Distinguished Professor of Meteorology, 503 Walker Building, University Park, PA, 16802.

CHAPTER 1

1. Bohren, Craig F. Understanding Colors in Nature, *Earth & Mineral Sciences.* 59(3):25-30; 1990.

CHAPTER 2

1. Strunk, William Jr., and White, E.B. *The Elements of Style.* New York: Macmillan Publishing Co., Inc. 1979. 92 pp.

CHAPTER 3

1. Bolander, Donald O., Dougherty, Margaret M., and Fitzgerald, Julia H. eds. *Instant Spelling Dictionary.* Chicago, Illinois: Career Institute Inc. 1964. 320 pp.

CHAPTER 4

1. Robert L. Bates. *Writing in Earth Science.* Published by the American Geological Institute, Alexandria, Virginia. 1988. 50 pp.

CHAPTER 5

1. Hagen, Wm. and staff, Branch of Editorial Services. *Bureau of Mines Manuscript Style Guide.* Washington, D.C.: U.S. Department of Interior. 1983. 152 pp.

CHAPTER 9

1. Costa, John, and Sylvester, Art. Comments, *Geological Society of America Bulletin.* 101(9):1105-1106; Sept. 1989.

2. Costa, John, and Sylvester, Art. Comments, *Geological Society of America Bulletin.* 102(7):851; July 1990.

3. Gopen, George D., and Swan, Judith A. The Science of Scientific Writing, *American Scientist.* 78(6):550-558; Nov.-Dec. 1990.

4. Tichy, Henrietta J. Advice to Scientist-Writers: Beware Old 'Fallacies,' *The Scientist.* 2(20):17-18; Oct. 31, 1988.

5. Mumpton, Frederick A. The Universal Recipe, Or How To Get Your Manuscript Accepted By Persnickety Editors, *Clays and Clay Minerals.* 38(6):631-636;1990.

Index

A

abbreviations, state, 133

abstracts

  descriptive abstracts, 10—12

  in scientific reports, 24—25, 162—163

"accept," use of term, 71

acceptance, letter of, 131, 140

acknowledgement letters, 131, 139

acknowledgements sections of reports, 28, 167—168

acronyms, pluralizing, 80

action words, 123—124

active verbs, use of, 41—43

active voice

  active/passive dilemma, 43—45

  use of, 45—46, 158, 159

activities sections in resumes, 121

address sections in resumes, 119

"Advice to Scientist Writers: Beware Old Fallacies," 149, 157—160

aerospace engineering, library resources for, 114

"affect," use of term, 71—72

AGI Glossary of Geology, 154

agricultural engineering, library resources for, 115

"alot," use of term, 72

"alright," use of term, 72

"alternate," use of term, 72

"alternative," use of term, 72

American National Standard for the Preparation of Scientific Papers for Written or Oral Presentation, 159

American Scientist, 156

"among," use of term, 72

"amount of," use of term, 73

amplification, transition words for, 40

anatomy, writing across the curriculum resources for, 170

"and"

  beginning sentences with, 159

  commas before, 60

  in subject/verb agreement, 35, 36

annotated bibliographies, 8—10

apostrophes, adding an "s" to a number or acronym with, 80

appendices in scientific reports, 28

Applied Science and Technology Index, 103

Arabic system of outlining, 7

architectural engineering, library resources for, 115

"architecture," use of term, 155—156

"area," use of term, 73

"as," use of term, 73

"aspects," use of word, 48
"assure," use of term, 73
astronomy, library resources for, 113
author-year system of source documentation, 97—99

B
Bates, Robert L., 71, 153
"between"
  "between ... and," use of term, 74
  use of term, 72
bibliographies, 101
  annotated, 8—10
"Bibliography of Additional Journal Articles About Writing, A," 150, 169—173
biology, writing across the curriculum resources for, 170
blind cover letters, 135, 136
"bundle," use of term, 155
Bureau of Mines Style Guide, 83
business, writing across the curriculum resources for, 170
"but," beginning sentences with, 159

C
"can," use of word, 47—48
capitalization, 61—63
captions, for figures and tables, 85—86
causality, transition words for, 40
chemistry and chemical engineering
  library resources for, 111
  writing across the curriculum resources for, 169—173
Chicago Manual of Style, 153
"cite," use of term, 74
civil engineering, library resources for, 115
Clays and Clay Minerals, 164, 169
closure, transition words for, 40
colons, 57—58
  with quotation marks, correct placement of, 56
commas, 58—61
  before "and," 60
  quotation marks and, 56
"Comments From Some Miffed Editors," 149, 150—153
"compare to," use of term, 74
"compare with," use of term, 74
"compose," use of term, 74—75
"compression" (geologic), use of term, 151, 156
"comprise"
  use of term, 75, 151
concession, transition words for, 41
concision, precision, revision (CPR), 33—35
conclusions
  citing sources in, 94
  in scientific reports, 27—28, 167
  in term papers, 22—23
"constitute," use of term, 74—75

"constrain," use of term, 151
"constriction" (geologic), use of term, 151
"continual," use of term, 75
"continuous," use of term, 75
"contraction" (geologic), use of term, 151
contractions, use of, 52—53
contrast, transition words for, 41
cover letters
  basics of formulating, 131—133
  samples of, 134—137
CPR (concision, precision, revision), 33—35

D
dangling modifiers, avoiding, 51—52
dashes, 58
dashes with quotation marks, correct placement of, 56
data
  "datum/data," use of, 151, 154
  presenting, in a report, 165—166
Day, Robert A., 169
decimal system of outlining, 6—7
decline, letter of, 131
degree measures of temperature, expressing, 53
Dennis, Patrick, 71
descriptive abstracts, style for, 10—12
detail, transition words for, 40
"different from," use of term, 75
"different than," use of term, 75
direction, writing about, 154
discussion sections in scientific reports, 166—167
distance, writing about, 154
documenting sources. *See* sources

E
earth science, library resources for, 107
editors
  comments on work submitted, 149, 150—156
  suggestions by, 150—156
education sections in resumes, 120
"effect," use of term, 71—72
e.g., use of, 75—76
Einstein, Albert, 81, 117
electrical engineering, library resources for, 114
Elements of Style, The (Strunk and White), 33—35, 104
"elongation" (geologic), use of term, 151
emphasis, transition words for, 40
employment sections in resumes, 120—121
endnotes, 101
Engineered Report Writing, 153
engineering
  library resources for, 106
  writing across the curriculum resources for, 171, 173

"ensure," use of term, 73

environmental engineering, library resources for, 115

equations, 81—83

essays. *See* term papers

"essentially," use of term, 151

et. al., use of, 75—76

etc., use of, 76

"Even More Comments From The Same Miffed Editors," 153—156

"evidence," use of term, 151

example, transition words for, 41

"except," use of term, 71

exclamation points with quotation marks, correct placement of, 56

experience sections in resumes, 120—121

experimental sections of scientific reports, 26, 165

"extension" (geologic), use of term, 151

F

"fabric" (geologic), use of term, 155

"facies" (geologic), use of term, 154

"fact," use of term, 76

"factor," use of term, 76

"farther," use of term, 76, 154

faults (geologic), writing about, 154

"feelings," use of word, 50

"fewer," use of term, 76—77

figures

  capitalization of, 61, 84

  captions for, 85—86

  functions of, 83

  fundamentals for, 86

  sample, 87—88

  in scientific reports, 24

  in term papers, 20

  treatment in text, 84

Forbes, Malcolm, 5

format for scientific reports, 23—28, 160—169

  abstracts, 24—25, 162—163

  acknowledgements, 28, 167—168

  appendices, 28

  authorship, 162

  conclusions, 22—23, 167

  data, presenting, 166—167

  discussion sections, 27, 166—167

  experimental sections, 26, 165

  introductions, 25, 163—165

  literature reviews, 25—26

  methods sections, 26

  organization as key, 160—161

  problem, stating the, 164

  procedures sections, 26

  references, 28, 168

  results sections, 27, 165—166

summary, 167
tenses, use of, 167
title, 161—162
"from ... to," use of term, 74
"further," use of term, 76, 154
future tense, 38

G
Geological Society of American Bulletin, 150, 153
Gopen, George D., 156
graduate school application essays, 131, 141—144
samples of, 143, 144
graduate student resumes, 122, 129—130
grammar checkers, use of, 64
graphics
equations, 81—83
figures. (*see* figures)
overuse of, 81
tables. (*see* tables)
greetings in professional letters, 132

H
halftone illustrations, use of, 166
headings
in memos, 18—19
in professional letters, 132
sections, in term papers, 22
Hill, Mason, 154
honors sections in resumes, 121
"however," beginning sentences with, 159
How to Write and Publish a Scientific Paper (Day), 169
hyphens, 56—57
"hypothesis," use of term, 153
"hypothesize," use of term, 151

I
"I," use of, 159
i.e., use of, 75
"imply," use of term, 77
"include," use of term, 74—75
industrial engineering, library resources for, 115
"infer," use of term, 77
infinitives, split, 52
"insure," use of term, 73
intention, transition words for, 40
"in terms of," use of phrase, 77
internship
blind cover letter for an, sample, 136
resume for an, sample, 125
interpretation, transition words for, 40
interviews
reasons for rejection, 147

tips for, 117, 147
introductions
  citing sources in, 94
  in reports, 25, 163—165
  in term papers, 20—21
"irregardless," use of term, 77
"is dependent upon," use of phrase, 153
"it," use of word, 49—50
"its," use of term, 77—78
"it's," use of term, 77—78

J
job objectives sections in resumes, 119
job offers
  acceptance, sample letter of, 140
  acknowledgement, sample letter of, 139
job seekers, reasons for rejection, 147
Johnson, Jess, 154
journal articles. *See* format for scientific reports; scientific reports

L
"lay," use of term, 78
"lead," use of term, 78
"led," use of term, 78
"less," use of term, 76—77
library resources. *See also* writing across the curriculum resources
  aerospace engineering, 114
  agricultural engineering, 115
  architectural engineering, 115
  astronomy, 113
  basics of using, 103—104
  chemistry and chemical engineering, 111
  civil engineering, 115
  earth science, 107
  electrical engineering, 114
  environmental engineering, 115
  industrial engineering, 115
  life science, 110
  material science, 108
  mathematical science, 112
  mechanical engineering, 114
  mineral economics and mineral engineering, 109
  nuclear engineering, 114
  physics, 113
  science and engineering, 106
  style manuals, 105, 153
"lie," use of term, 78
life science, library resources for, 110
"like," use of term, 73
lines (geologic), writing about, 152
location, transition words for, 40

M

manuscripts. *See* format for scientific reports; scientific reports
masculine form, use of, 50—51
material science, library resources for, 108
mathematics
   library resources for, 112
"may," use of term, 78
McGraw-Hill Style Manual, The, 104
measured quantities, expressing, 53
medicine, writing across the curriculum resources for, 172
memos
   parts of, 18—19
   sample, 18—20
   writing, 18—20
methods sections in scientific reports, 26
"might," use of term, 78
mineral economics and mineral engineering, library resources for, 109
Murray, Melba, 153
music, writing across the curriculum resources for, 172
"myself," use of term, 155

N

name sections in resumes, 119
narrative approach to graduate school application essays, 141, 144
notes, references and, 101
nouns
   capitalization and, 61—63
   forming plurals, 150, 151, 154, 155
   possessives, 152, 153
   singular/plural pairs, tricky, 36—37
   stringing together, 152
   subject/verb agreement, 35—36
nuclear engineering, library resources for, 114
"number of," use of term, 73
numbers
   pluralizing, 80
   textual references to, 53

O

objectives
   sections in resumes, 119
   in term papers, 21
"occur," use of term, 151
"occurrence," use of term, 151
"one," use of term, 78—79
oral reports, 28—31
   guidelines from professional organizations for, 28, 30
   visual aids in, 30
organizations, citing references from, 98, 100
outlines
   mechanics of outlining, 6—7
   sample outline, 7—8

systems of outlining, 6—7
value of, 6
overused words, 47—50

P
"packages," use of term, 152—153, 155
"packets," use of term, 152—153, 155
paragraphs
  integrating sources in, 94—96
  writing good, 38—39
"part," use of term, 151
passive voice
  active/passive dilemma, 43—45
  use of, 46—47, 158, 159—160
past tense, 37—38
"per," use of term, 79
"percent," use of term, 79
"percentage," use of term, 79
perfect tense, 38
periods with quotation marks, correct placement of, 56
personal pronouns, use of, 159—160
phenomena, active verbs that describe, 42—43
physics
  library resources for, 113
  writing across the curriculum resources for, 169—173
physiology, writing across the curriculum resources for, 170
plagiarism, 91, 92
plural nouns, forming, 150, 151, 154, 155
plural/singular pairs, tricky, 36—37
Poincaré, Jules Henri, 103
"portion," use of term, 151
possessives, 152, 153
"postulate," use of term, 151—152
precision, 33—34
prepositions, ending sentences with, 158—159
present tense, 37
"pretty," use of term, 79
"principal," use of term, 79
"principle," use of term, 79
"prior to," use of term, 153
problem in scientific reports, stating the, 164
procedures sections in scientific reports, 26
professional activities sections in resumes, 121
professional letters
  basics of formulating, 131—133
  graduate school application essays, 131, 141—144
  recommendation letters, requesting, 145—146
  samples, 134—144
progress reports
  sample report, 17—18
  style for, 16—17
  value of, 15—16

pronouns, personal
  in progress reports, 16
  in proposals, 14
  use of, 159—160
proposals
  effective, 12
  pitfalls of, 13
  sample, 14—15
  style for, 13—14
ProQuest, 104

Q
quality of writing
  editors' comments on, 149, 150—156
  improving, 156—157
query letter, 131
question marks with quotation marks, correct placement of, 56
"quite," use of term, 79
quotation marks, 56
quotations, citing, 43

R
"rather," use of term, 79
Reader's Guide to Periodical Literature, 104
recommendation letters, requesting, 145—146
references. *See also* sources
  citing, 168
  pages
    author-year system of documentation, 97—98
    fundamentals for, 101
    number system of documentation, 99—101
  in proposals, 15
  in resumes, 118
  in scientific reports, 28, 168
  in term papers, 23
  for writing across the curriculum, 169—173
"region," use of term, 73
rejection, reasons for, 147
reports
  author's responsibility in, 153—154, 157
  data, presenting, 165—166
  format for. (*see* format for scientific reports)
  improving style for writing, 156—157
  oral. (*see* oral reports)
  progress. (*see* progress reports)
  resources on style for, 104—105, 153
  reviewing, 168—169
  scientific. (*see* format for scientific reports; scientific reports)
  submission requirements, 168
  technical. (*see* format for scientific reports; scientific reports)
  tenses in, 167
research approach to graduate school application essays, 141, 143
resources library. (*see* library resources)

style, 104—105, 153
for writing across the curriculum. (*see* writing across the curriculum resources)
"respective," use of term, 79—80
"respectively," use of term, 79—80
results sections in scientific reports, 27, 165—166
resumes
    action words for, 123—127
    graduate student, 122, 129—130
    mechanical guidelines for writing, 118—119
    samples of, 125—130
    sections in, 119—122
revision, 33—35

S
Salvador, Amos, 154
sample(s)
    annotated bibliography, 9—10
    cover letters, 134—137
    descriptive abstracts, 11—12
    equation, 83
    figure, 87—88
    graduate school application essays, 143, 144
    job offer
        acceptance, letter of, 140
        acknowledgement, letter of, 139
    memos, 18—20
    outline, 7—8
    progress reports, 17—18
    proposal, 14—15
    references page for
        author-year system of documentation, 98—99
        number system of documentation, 100—101
    resumes, 125—130
    table, 88—89
    thank you letter, 138
"scenario," use of term, 153
Schnabel, Diane, 169
science
    library resources for, 106
    writing across the curriculum resources for, 173
scientific reports. *See also* reports
    format for (*see* format for scientific reports)
    mechanics, 24
    organization as key, 160—161
    references, 28, 168
    reviewing, 168—169
    submission requirements, 168
    tenses, use of, 167
Scientist, The, 157
"section," use of term, 73
"sediments," use of term, 152

selected bibliography, 101
semicolons, 57—58
  with quotation marks, correct placement of, 56
sentences
  beginning, 159
  construction of, 157—159
  ending, with prepositions, 158—159
  linking, 38—39
  topic, 39—40
  transition words for, 40—41
sexist language, avoiding, 50—51
Shepard, R.A., 169
"shortening" (geologic), use of term, 151
"show," use of term, 151, 152, 154
"sight," use of term, 74
similarity, transition words for, 40
"since," use of term, 152
singular/plural pairs, tricky, 36—37
"site," use of term, 74
skills cover letter, 137
Smith, Sydney, 33
sociology, writing across the curriculum resources for, 172—173
sources. *See also* references
  in annotated bibliographies, 8—9
  basics of using, 92—93
  integration of, 94—96
  mandatory citation of, 91—92
  in memos, 19
  in proposals, 14—15
  references pages
    author-year system of documentation, 97—98
    fundamentals of, 98, 100, 101
    number system of documentation, 99—101
  in term papers, 23
speaking, oral reports and, 28—30
"spectra," as plural form, 151
spell checkers, use of, 63—64
spelling
  rules, 64—66
  terminology commonly misspelled, 69—70
  words commonly misspelled, 66—68
split infinitives, avoiding, 52
"s / 's," use of, 80
states, two-letter abbreviations for, 133
strain (geologic), 151, 155
"strata," as plural form, 151
stress (geologic), 151, 155
"structure" (geologic), use of term, 155—156
Strunk, William, Jr., 33—35
style
  editors' comments on, 149, 150—156
  improving, 156—157

resources, 105, 153
subjectivity in writing evaluation, 33
subject/verb agreement, 35—36
submission requirements for manuscripts, 168
"suggest," use of term, 151—152
Suggestions to Authors of Reports of the U.S. Geological Survey, 153
summary sections in reports, 167
"superimpose," use of term, 155
"superpose," use of term, 155
surfaces (geologic), writing about, 152
Swan, Judith A., 156

T
tables
    capitalization of, 61, 84
    captions for, 85—86
    functions of, 83
    fundamentals for, 86—87
    in scientific reports, 24, 166
    in term papers, 20
    treatment in text, 84—87
tailored cover letter, 134
teaching approach to graduate school application essays, 141
technical reports. *See* format for scientific reports; scientific reports
temperature
    expressing degree measures of, 53
    scales, capitalization of, 63
"tension" (geologic), use of term, 151
term papers
    body of, 22
    introductions in, 20—21
    mechanics of, 20
    objectives in, 21
    section headings used in, 22
    thesis statements in, 21
    title, 20
thank you letters, 131
    sample letter, 138
"that," use of term, 80
thesis statements in term papers, 21
"this," use of word, 49—50
Tichey, Henrietta, J., 157
time
    transition words for, 41
    writing about, 152
title, report, 161—162
"to be," use of term, 152
transition words, use of, 40
"try and," use of term, 80

U

"Universal Recipe, or How to Get Your Manuscript Accepted By Persnickety Editors," 160

"Universal Recipe for Scientific Reports, The," 150, 160—169

V

vagueness, avoiding, 150, 151, 154, 168—169

verbs
  active verbs, use of, 41—42
  verb/subject agreement, 35—36

verb tenses, 37—38
  in annotated bibliographies, 8
  in descriptive abstracts, 11
  in proposals, 13—14
  in reports, 167
  in scientific report discussion sections, 27

"very," use of term, 79

visual aids in oral reports, 30

voice
  active, 45—46, 158, 159
  active/passive dilemma, 43—45
  passive, 46—47, 158, 159

W

"we," use of, 25, 159

"whereas," use of term, 152

"which," use of term, 80

White, E.B., 33—35

"will," use of word, 47—48

"would," use of word, 47—48

writing
  editors' comments on quality of, 149, 150—156
  improving, 156—157
  resources. (see library resources; resources; writing across the curriculum resources)
  resources for, 169—173
  subjective evaluation and, 33
  unlearning old fallacies about, 157—160

writing across the curriculum resources. See also library resources
  anatomy, 170
  biology, 170
  business, 170
  chemistry, 170—171
  engineering, 171, 173
  mathematics, 171—172
  medicine, 172
  music, 172
  nursing, 172
  physics, 172
  physiology, 170
  science, 173
  sociology, 172—173

Writing in Earth Science, 71, 153
writing-intensive courses
   characteristics of, 5
   surviving, 5—32

Y
"you," use of term, 25, 78—79
"young" (verb), use of term, 154